IKE KLIGERMAN BARKLEY
HOUSES

IKE KLIGERMAN BARKLEY
HOUSES

FOREWORD BY ROBERT A. M. STERN

TEXT WRITTEN IN COLLABORATION WITH MARC KRISTAL

THE MONACELLI PRESS

Library of Congress Cataloging-in-Publication Data

Ike Kligerman Barkley (Firm).

Ike Kligerman Barkley : houses / foreword by Robert A. M. Stern ; written in collaboration with Marc Kristal.

p. cm.

ISBN 978-1-58093-269-1

1. Ike Kligerman Barkley (Firm). 2. Architecture, Domestic—United States. 3. Architecture—United States—History—20th century. 4. Architecture—United States—History—21st century. I. Stern, Robert A. M. II. Kristal, Marc. III. Title.

NA737.I38A4 2010

728′.370922—dc22   2009041952

Printed in China

www.monacellipress.com

10 9 8 7 6 5 4 3 2 1
First edition

Designed by Doug Turshen with David Huang

CONTENTS

FOREWORD
ROBERT A. M. STERN

THE WORK IN THIS BOOK REFLECTS a sea change that has taken place in American architecture over the past twenty years or so, a change that has reopened the discourse between the new and what went before. This discourse was denied to practicing architects for fifty years or more by the schismatic polemic of stylistic modernism that deemed the past a closed book and the present little more than a launching point for the future.

I've known John Ike, Thomas Kligerman, and Joel Barkley since they were students of mine (Ike and Kligerman) and valued members of my office (all three). They are not theorists or polemicists: they are gifted practitioners of the art of architecture. They build for the here and now but are at home in architecture's history, from which their work gains its strength; they speak architectural languages of the past with a sure command of grammar and syntax and a rich vocabulary of form and detail. As designers they build upon what went before to extend the trajectory of architecture. Commenting on the past, they say new things.

George Kubler, in his 1962 book *The Shape of Time,* one of the most important meditations on the nature of art and its history, talks about the timing of artistic entrances into the stream of culture. Some artists, though very gifted, find themselves out of step with their time. Ike, Kligerman, and Barkley entered into independent practice at just the right time: not only were potential clients hungering for new work that resonated with tradition, but there were also other young architects, and a few older, more established ones as well, who shared the new firm's enthusiasm for a discourse enriched by the broadest possible engagement with the discipline. As the three architects entered partnership and independent practice in the late 1980s, there was for the first time in a generation or more a support culture for a synthesis of traditional form with modern programs and building techniques.

The groundwork for the traditionalism that emerged in the 1980s was set down by the postmodernism of the 1960s and 1970s. Modern traditionalists like Ike, Kligerman, and Barkley came on the scene just as the giddy naughtiness of early postmodernism's play with history was being supplanted by a deeper, more resonant investigation of the past fueled by fresh scholarship that renewed appreciation of neglected master architects like Sir Edwin Lutyens and Harrie T. Lindeberg, to name but two of many who were being "rediscovered." That scholarship also drew attention to the diversity and regional variation architecture had enjoyed in the United States and elsewhere before it fell beneath the totalizing juggernaut of stylistic modernism, which had underpinnings in a pseudoscientific functionalism and an overheated evaluation of technology. With the rise of a "new traditionalism," it was again possible for architects to design differently as they confronted different places, programs, local cultures, and client aspirations.

The work in this book is wonderfully consistent in quality and also wonderfully inconsistent in style. It is eclectic, a term that suffers from misinterpretation and abuse but that has a long and admirable history going back deep into the modern tradition. Eclecticism is fundamental to modernity, a way of thinking and doing that enables creative people to synthesize the best from the past in order to go forward in culture.

As seen in these pages, Ike, Kligerman, and Barkley pursue an eclecticism of taste, homing in on the forms of one period or one master in any given house they design. But there is also the possibility of an eclecticism of style that, encompassing a mix of elements, has within it the capacity for a new synthesis. Such may not be the interest of these architects, at least not yet. But given the sure command of form that they exhibit, it is certainly a direction their work may take them. That aside, for the present and foreseeable future, what they do is more than enough: an architecture that is free of cant, inventive, culturally connected, and broadly accessible. And that is a lot to have accomplished in the first twenty years of a still young practice.

INTRODUCTION
JOHN IKE, THOMAS KLIGERMAN, JOEL BARKLEY

WHEN ASKED TO DESCRIBE THE IKE KLIGERMAN BARKLEY philosophy of practice, we typically cite contextualism—that is, the architectural precedents that surround a given project, coupled with the qualities of the site—as our primary consideration. Underlying this relatively straightforward approach, however, are factors that, across nearly twenty-five years and some 250 projects, have both directed our work and shaped its particular nature.

The first is our love of collaboration. Because almost all of IKBA's work is residential, every project represents a highly personal journey in the course of which we endeavor to translate a client's needs, tastes, and aspirations into a true, individual home. The success of that journey depends on our ability to communicate. Thus the firm's preference for working in a range of historic styles (including, when appropriate, twentieth-century Modernism) represents not just a response to context but the need for a shared architectural language—one that our clients can readily embrace.

Working in the styles of the past does not preclude personal expression. Just as novelists and filmmakers gravitate toward genres that suit the themes they choose to explore, we look for the historic style that represents the best vehicle for the architectural story we wish to tell. Moreover, each of the firm's principals has a unique way of working and ideas, themes, and obsessions that are ever-changing and evolving—burrs that stick in the creative conscience and manifest themselves in every project, no matter the genre.

Yet despite this diversity, there is a consistency to IKBA's designs, one that derives from a classical approach to detail. What this means, in practical terms, is that every project is the outcome of a comprehensive investigation into the underpinnings of its governing style, one that looks at how specific

elements were originally designed and crafted, and why certain aesthetic choices were made. Synthesizing these details and ideas into a unified whole remains one of the hallmarks of the firm's work—and, we believe, marks the difference between superficial pastiche and a fully realized work of architecture.

This pleasure in research and depth of understanding also drives IKBA's particular brand of innovation: the unusual, sometimes unlikely, mixing of styles. When there are multiple references upon which to draw, or the local architecture proves unsuitable, or married clients propose opposing ideas, combining elements into a hybrid—such as the conflation of English Cottage and Shingle Style architecture we dubbed "Shinglish"—has, in our view, produced some of the firm's most successful designs. It also finds a precedent in the work of our favorite practitioners, including Stanford White, John Staub, Bernard Maybeck, Carlo Scarpa, George Howe, and Harrie T. Lindeberg—men who introduced modern building techniques and influences into traditional genres to produce memorable, original architecture.

Modernity, finally, remains key. IKBA is a contemporary practice, and many of our signature motifs—such as reducing houses to the depth of a single room, to maximize light, views, and air flow— derive from contemporary preferences. If the firm's projects are rich in architectural history, that history is embedded in modern buildings that satisfy the requirements of today's life.

And so what begins as contextualism arrives, we hope, as something more: an answering of a client's needs and an expression of a personal design vision; an appreciation of architectural history and the surprising ways in which styles can enrich each other; a traditional, thoroughly considered approach to detail, material, and craft coupled with an enthusiastic embrace of modernity. And most of all, a delight in architecture—in particular the uniquely complex, endlessly enriching object known as a house.

COUNTRYSIDE

ARTS AND CRAFTS COTTAGE

Michigan, 2003

THE FIRM WAS FORTUNATE TO HAVE, in a Michigan couple, clients interested in creating a home in which each room would manifest a particular character, one developed via an exploration of material and detail. In response, we looked to Michigan's Cranbrook Academy of Art, which, under the stewardship of its first director, Finnish architect Eliel Saarinen, had encouraged a holistic, craft-based approach to design. We combined our interest in the Cranbrook sensibility with our clients' affection for the English Arts and Crafts and Wiener Werkstätte movements to produce a residence that braids together multiple strands of decorative detail rendered in a rich palette of materials—almost all of them crafted by hand.

The exterior facades are finished in a diminutive, custom-fabricated brick that was set into a rhythmic complexity of patterns, most evidently on the massive gable dominating the entry facade. Carved limestone on the chimneys and window bays features classical egg-and-dart motifs and abstract rope profiles as well as fluted and scalloped details. Cast bronze was employed for the leaders and gutters; we established a hierarchy of patterns, involving differing scales and degrees of elaboration, for different parts of the house.

Multiple historic references were mined to embellish the interiors. The master bath, with its carved mahogany vanities and French Art Deco–influenced mosaic friezes formed from marble, alabaster, and onyx, takes its overall style from the Wiener Werkstätte. The sitting room features decorative marquetry inspired by the English Arts and Crafts architect Baillie Scott. In the dining room, the pattern of the vaulted ceiling, a motif borrowed from the Regency architect Sir John Soane, is echoed in the floor by a change of direction in the walnut boards. Every space is different. Yet rather than seeming cacophonous, the varied clusters of rooms are unified by the design's commitment to superlative materials and craftsmanship.

PREVIOUS PAGES: *The formal front facade of this residence features a compendium of craft-based elements, including custom-fabricated brick, carved limestone chimney details, and cast-bronze leaders and gutters.* OPPOSITE: *In keeping with the less formal rear facade, the landscaping is reflective of an English park.*

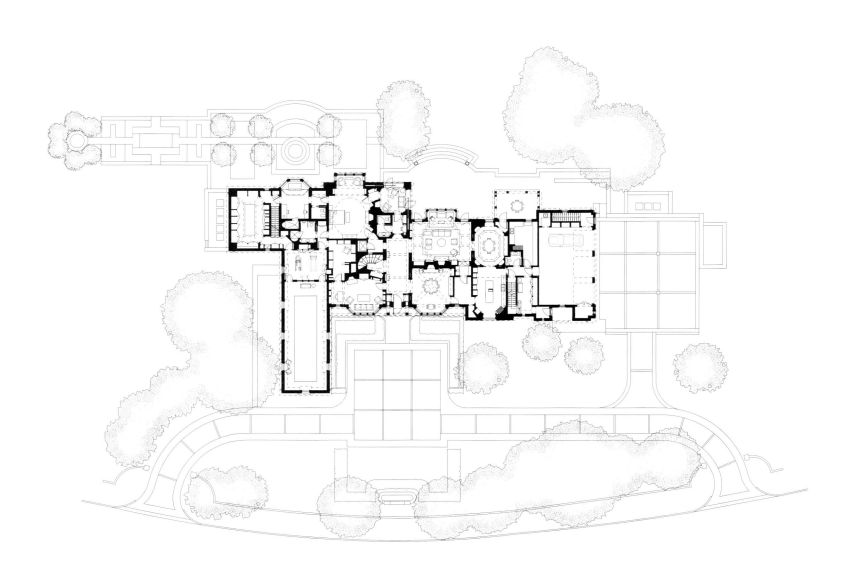

PREVIOUS PAGES: *Fin-de-siècle detailing in the entry's plaster and woodwork reflects the house's northern European influences. The restored leaded-glass windows date from the early twentieth century.* RIGHT: *The living room's octagonal cove ceiling was inspired by Sir Edwin Lutyens's design for Marsh Court at Hampshire.*

ABOVE: *The vaulted ceiling's pattern, a design borrowed from Sir John Soane, is restated in a change of direction in the floor boards.*
OPPOSITE: *In the library, which features Biedermeier and Austrian accessories and furnishings, the figure in the carpet is reflected in the plaster fretwork of the ceiling.*

SHINGLISH
COUNTRY HOUSE

New Jersey, 1993

THIS HOUSE, IN A NEW JERSEY SEASIDE COMMUNITY in which Mediterranean villas predominate, evolved from our client's willingness to embark on a stylistic experiment. Because the town had developed, early in the last century, around a core of public buildings evincing an English architectural influence and is a neighbor to Elberon, where McKim, Mead & White created some of their most notable Shingle Style houses, we suggested a hybrid of the two. The client agreed, and we characterize the result as "Shinglish."

Largely inspired by Folly Farm, Sir Edwin Lutyens's 1906 Cottage Style masterwork, the design is simultaneously earthbound and airborne. Below, massive curved buttresses, constructed from irregularly shaped clinker bricks, firmly anchor the composition. Above, the enormous, steeply sloping gabled roof—the tight wrapping of its shingled surface enhanced by an absence of trim—seems like a huge witch's cowl caught from beneath by the wind. This sense of weightlessness is heightened by the roof's "drunken weave" shingle patterns, flared edges, and arresting blackish-green stain.

With its light-filled, generously glazed rooms, the interior contravenes the expectations established by the dark and looming roof. The architecture continues the exterior's stylistic duality, with woven latticework screens derived from McKim, Mead & White precedents and Lutyensesque detailing, notably in the carved balusters of the oak stairwell. A note of modernity appears in the windows, all of which are constructed from identically sized, modular panes.

Outside, the firm zoned the one-acre property into a series of virtual "rooms" that reflects the plan and program of the interior. The yew-lined front green, narrow side yard, and hedge-bordered terraces effectively continue the spaces defined by the house's formal chambers. In back, a linear garden contains a more informal gathering space. And beyond this, we sited the largest "room" of all: the pool, overlooked by a garage/cabana that resembles the house in miniature.

PREVIOUS PAGES: *This New Jersey residence combines a steeply sloping Shingle Style roof with English Cottage Style brick buttresses, resulting in a "Shinglish" hybrid.* OPPOSITE: *The house's irregularly shaped clinker bricks impart an overlay of craft and animate the surfaces of the strongly geometric forms.*

ABOVE: *The buttress shape of the house's massive piers was inspired by Sir Edwin Lutyens's 1906 Folly Farm. It is complemented by the entry's V-joint wood ceiling.*
OPPOSITE: *In the diminutive vestibule, "fish scale" shingles cover the walls, their delicacy balancing the bluestone floor.*

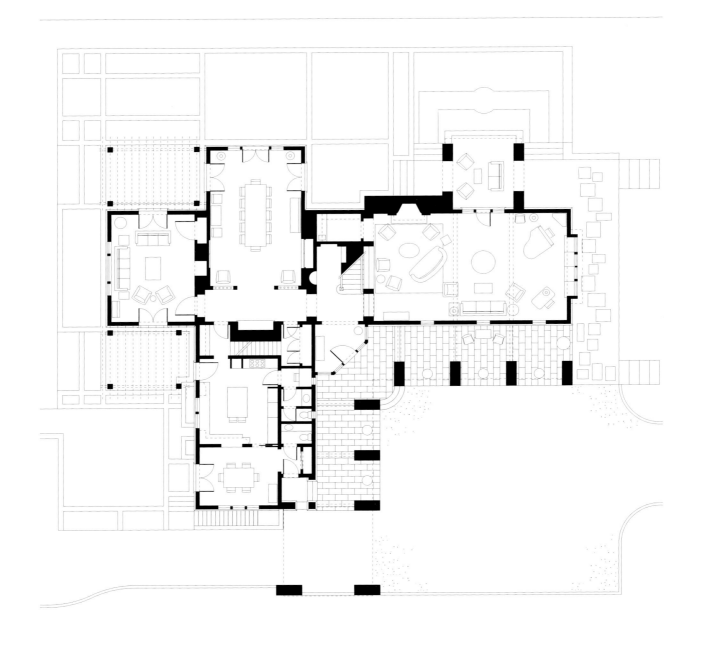

0   5   10   20 ft

ABOVE: *The acre-sized property is divided into a series of outdoor rooms that reflect the plan and program of the interior. The largest, facing the house's rear facade, contains the pool.*

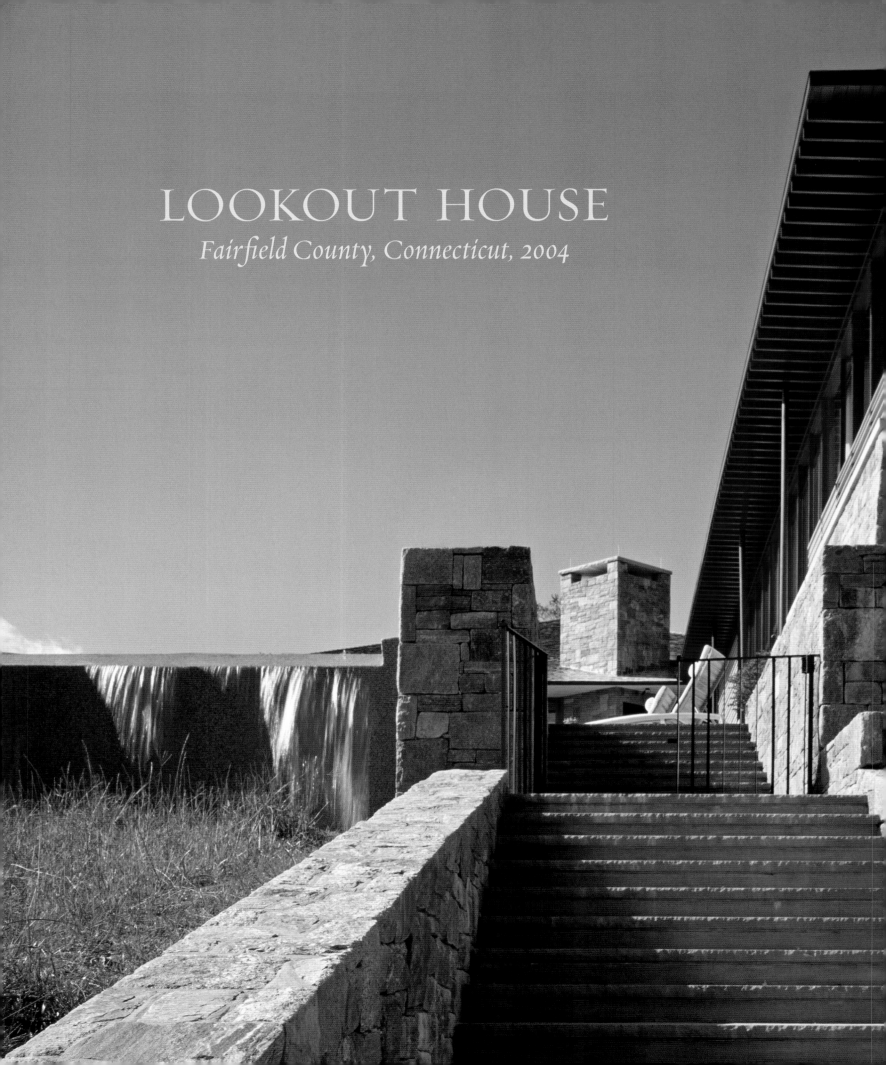

LOOKOUT HOUSE

Fairfield County, Connecticut, 2004

CREATING A HARMONIOUS RELATIONSHIP BETWEEN an existing house and a new addition is especially complicated when the residence takes the Platonic form of a pyramid. That is what we found on a dramatic hilltop site in southern Connecticut. Our clients chose to retain the eccentric and gloomy 1979 structure and commissioned a gut renovation and extension.

The pyramid, centered on an open-plan double-height living space surrounding an indoor pool, was lightened and simplified with a contemporary material palette (including bamboo, bluestone, and glass tile) and a new lighting program. Oppressive, outmoded structural members were stripped from the skylight, opening the interior to expansive views of Long Island Sound. Three small bedrooms were replaced by two more sizable ones for the owners' children.

We relocated the master suite to a new wing, along with a den, music studio, exercise room, staff quarters, and wine cellar. Enclosing these functions in volume that complemented, rather than competed with, the original structure proved to be one of the firm's biggest design challenges. The initial scheme took

the form of an upside-down pyramid—conceptually exciting but highly impractical. This was followed by one featuring a V-shaped roof—an echo of the first idea, though proportionally too large. Our third concept grew out of the recognition that despite its pyramidal roof, the structure had a strong horizontal component: a low band of encircling windows. We created a form that drew those windows out in a horizontal line, almost as though a sleek passenger train had departed from the house and traveled eastward, capturing the spectacular light and views. The addition's flat-roofed upper floor became the master suite, sitting on a plinth of tailored fieldstone, with which we also reclad the house.

A glass bridge—an "architectural synapse" that clearly differentiates old from new—connects the main house to the master suite. Like the original structure, the suite is essentially a large volume enclosing a smaller one—in this case, a freestanding cube, finished in claro walnut, that divides the sleeping and bath areas. This structure also reinforces the architecture's strong linear character by pushing straight through the suite to the out of doors where, clad in copper, it forms the back wall of a private terrace.

37

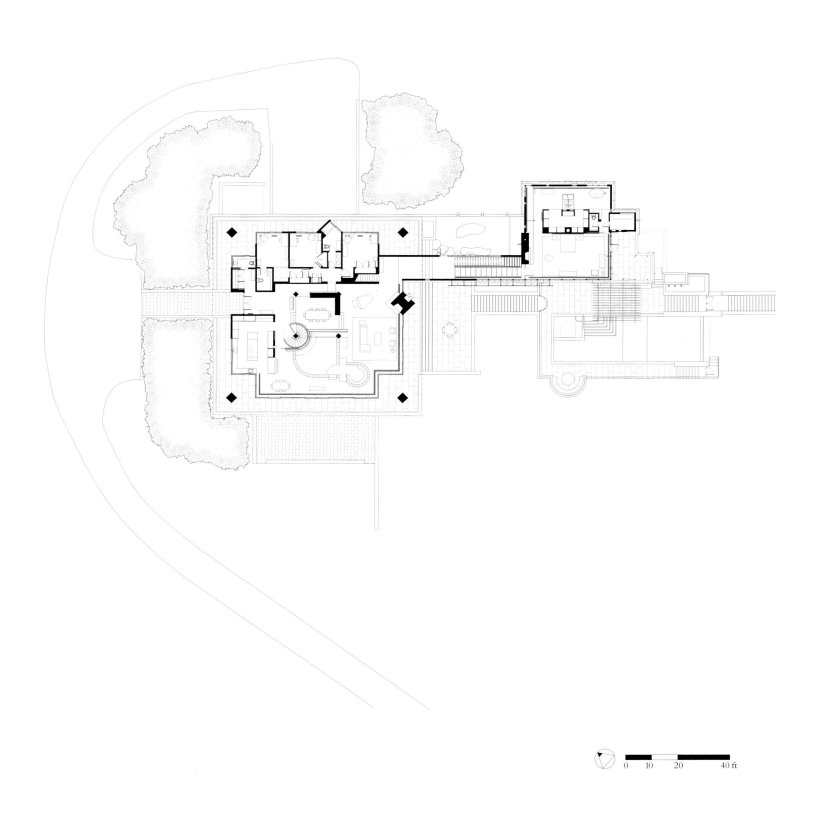

0 10 20 40 ft

LEFT: *In the master bedroom, a double-sided mirror floats between his-and-hers sinks.*
OPPOSITE: *A freestanding claro walnut cabinet separates sleeping and bathing areas in the master suite. The volume continues onto the terrace, enclosing the shower.*

RIGHT: *The original house features a double-height, open-plan living space overlooking an indoor pool. The renovation included a new skylight lighting plan and material palette.*

WOODLAND RAMBLE

Redding, Connecticut, 1998

THIS DESIGN MINES ARCHITECTURAL HISTORY to resolve contradictory desires: for an old-fashioned residence reflective of the owners' contemporary design sensibility; for a private getaway that also welcomes guests; and for the refined pleasures of Connecticut country living on a reasonable budget. During an initial discussion, our clients expressed a fondness for the ad hoc layout of farmhouses as well as for Shingle Style design; these references sparked a memory of a 1937 Bay Area residence by the California architect Bernard Maybeck. A sculptural composition of linked volumes rendered in concrete and corrugated iron, Maybeck's creation at once looks backward to English manor architecture and breaks ground with its choice of materials and juxtaposition of forms.

In that spirit, the firm developed a shingle-wrapped residence consisting of three connected structures—the main house, a middle volume for guests, and a garage/sleeping loft—that updates the classic farmhouse via a freestyle treatment of the undulating roofline that unites the multiple forms. By locating visitors in a separate wing, the plan preserves the owners' privacy. And the design's reliance on visual drama, rather than expensive materials, to deliver architectural interest answered our clients' desire for a home that is both accessible and affordable.

Part of the drama derives from a play on scale. The main house's voluminous great room, with its expanses of glass and peaked ceiling, contrasts with the tiny semicircular library tucked behind it. Outside, between the double-height corner windows that define the rear of the guest wing, the roof swoops sharply downward, stopping above a low wall pierced only by a porthole. In addition, the design creates interest by confounding expectation. To modulate the scale of the living room, surfaces were covered with four-by-eight-foot sheets of birch plywood, the seams hidden with a discreet trim that outlines the doors as well—a simple, economical way to add texture and warmth where neither is typically found.

We also created a formal entry procession—a long pergola, supported by twin rows of stone piers, stretches from the garage to the front door—to enclose a lawn. This courtyard, overlooked by all three structures, offers a protected outdoor view, contrasting with the more exposed landscape surrounding the house.

PREVIOUS PAGES: *Three linked structures expand a simple house for two into a rambling family retreat. The arrangement of garage, guest wing, and main house creates and surrounds a cloistered inner court.*
OPPOSITE: *Windows grouped at a corner flood the interior with sunlight and mediate between the monumental window bay and the intimate bedroom.*

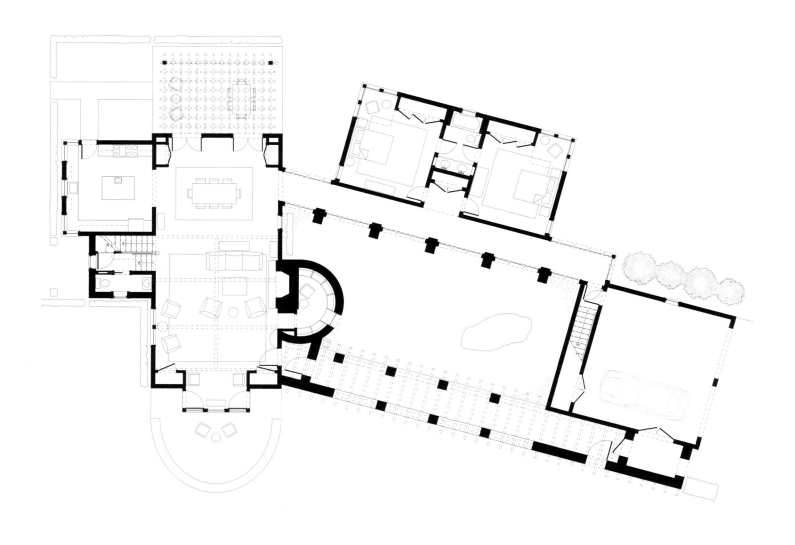

0   5   10   20 ft

ABOVE: *The undulating roofline unites the three wings.*
In a witty contrast, stately double-height bay windows flank
a cedar-shingled wall pierced only by a diminutive oculus.

ABOVE AND OPPOSITE: *A long pergola, supported by twin rows of stone piers and terminating in a boldly colored front door, serves as a formal entry procession. The pergola also encloses a lawn, overlooked by all three of the house's volumes.*

RIGHT: *The great room employs an unexpectedly modest wall treatment: off-the-shelf sheets of birch plywood ashed with white stain and outlined by simple strips of maple.*

GREEN SPRINGS FARM

Louisa, Virginia, 2004

THIS 6,500-SQUARE-FOOT COUNTRY SEAT commands a knoll atop a thousand-acre horse farm in the Green Springs National Historic Landmark District, in Louisa County, Virginia. Most of Green Springs's historic houses are symmetrical structures reflective of the classical tradition's ideal forms. Yet our clients, a passionate horsewoman and her garden-loving husband, wanted a working farm (including a twenty-eight-stall barn), which suggested a farmhouse more appealingly ad hoc. The task was to reconcile these opposites in a design that united the formal propriety of the region's architectural history with a farm's wild, untamed nature.

Considering the hilltop site, the firm turned for inspiration to the Acropolis, envisioning a loose assemblage of white Greek Revival volumes atop a vast landscape of green. This strategy enabled us to have it both ways, incorporating the iconic formal elements of a traditional southern home into an informal, rambling plan, one that gives equal weight to the house's private, social, and utilitarian spaces.

The introduction to the house is indeed formal: a symmetrical, columned portico leads to a grand entry hall paved with black-and-white checkered marble, which opens into a library measuring thirteen by thirteen by thirteen feet. Yet because, in a farmhouse, it is the kitchen that is in the middle of everything, we placed that room at the center of the overall composition, where it enjoys the best view. The layout, which reflects the typical stop-and-start construction history of most farm buildings, also generated a lively variety of forms, each shaped to its particular function. And because the concept was flexible enough to embrace a range of architectural influences, unexpected elements, like the outdoor gallery off the second-floor guest rooms (seen typically in homes farther south), found their way into the design as well.

Along with the copper roof, which has patinated to a lustrous golden brown (on its way to verdigris), the house is unified by its white-painted materials—stucco, clapboard, brick, and shiplap. While there is a correlation between exterior treatment and interior function that suggests a hierarchy of importance (the core structures are stucco, the appendages are clad in clapboard), the range of textures produces an overlay of surface animation and allows the buildings to weather differently—a condition entirely appropriate to a working farm.

PREVIOUS PAGES: *The design incorporates the forms of a classical home into the casual plan of a typical farmhouse.* OPPOSITE: *The house is sited on a thousand-acre horse farm.*

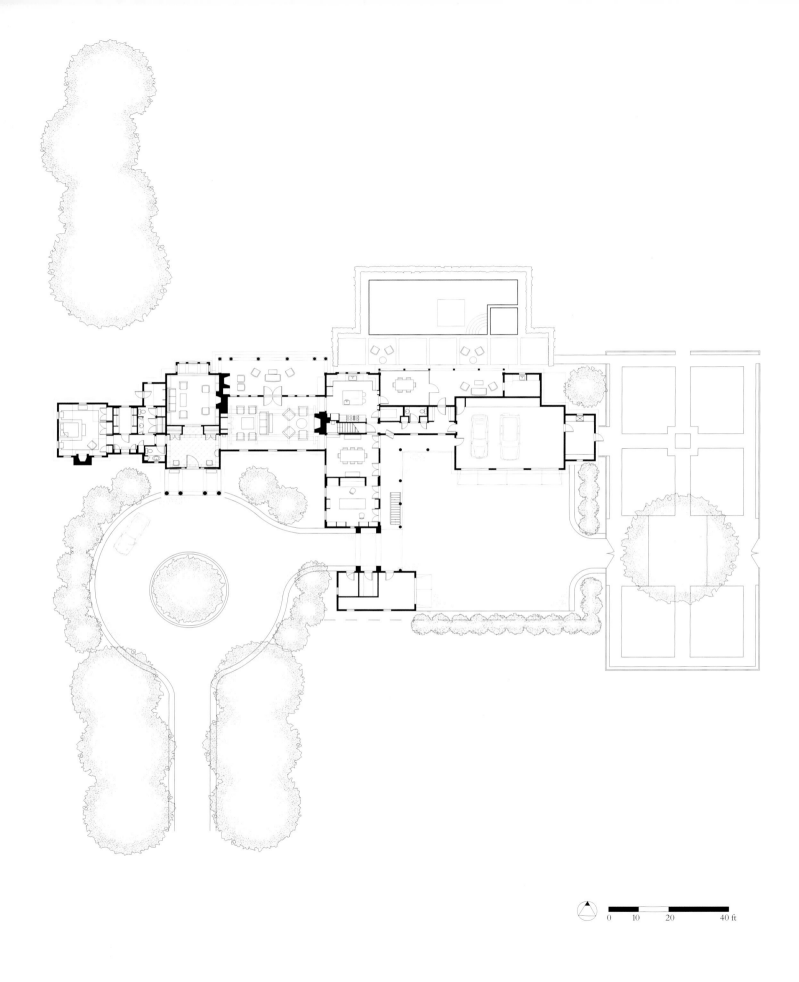

ABOVE: *The entry wing contains the most formal space in the house:*
a grand entry hall paved with black-and-white marble checkerboard.
OPPOSITE: *The entry hall opens into a richly hued library measuring*
thirteen by thirteen by thirteen feet—a perfect cube.

LEFT: *In addition to the house, the owners commissioned a twenty-eight-stall horse barn.* OPPOSITE: *The barn's central pavilion, with its steeply pitched roof—a dramatic contrast with the low-slung stable wings—draws on a Harrie T. Lindeberg design for a stable in Ohio.*

CLASSICAL HOUSE

New Jersey, 1999

THE AESTHETIC OF THIS NEW JERSEY RESIDENCE evolved from our clients' desire to build something that might stand as a legacy for their children and the family's future generations. While the oceanside community featured distinguished examples of Tudor, Shingle Style, and Mediterranean architecture, none of these seemed precisely right for a stately yet welcoming home within which memories and traditions might comfortably nest. As an alternative, the firm suggested the kind of classically influenced Colonial Revival country house popularized, at the turn of the last century, by such architects as Charles A. Platt and Harrie T. Lindeberg. This style seemed entirely appropriate to the site, on a well-established street with a rhythmic allée of stately London plane trees. The outcome is a house that, architecturally, proves at once entirely appropriate and locally unique.

Outside, the house reveals the particular mix of influences associated with the style: Colonial front and rear facades, Greek Revival double-story temple-front ends. Within, the generously scaled entry hall, its fireplace directly opposite the front door, establishes a tone of welcoming gentility. This is reinforced by the simplicity of the plan: upon arrival, a visitor finds the living room to one side, the dining room to the other, and a combined family and breakfast room straight ahead. While the second floor contains the principal private spaces, the house opens out again dramatically on the third level into a ninety-foot-long ballroom, illuminated from above by an expansive oculus.

The firm's interior design scheme reinforces the Colonial spirit. We combined craftwork, including the entry hall's hand-hooked rug and a wall-mounted quilt above the stair, with eighteenth-century antiques, principally tables, chests, and chairs. Furniture captures the essence of the period without sacrificing contemporary notions of comfort. And the dining room walls are lined with a reissue of the 1830s Zuber wallpaper "Scenes of North America," designed by Joseph Dufour, which recalls America's Arcadian past.

Working with the artist and color consultant Donald Kaufman, we developed an updated, freshened version of an eighteenth-century palette. While a lively series of hues, coordinated with the fabric selections, brighten the various rooms, it is the radiant yellow (tinged with green) on the exterior that captures the house's particular mix of historical precedent, familial embrace, and modern informality.

PREVIOUS PAGES: *To create a home that would stand as a legacy for future generations, the firm chose the classically influenced Colonial Revival style popularized in the early twentieth century.*
OPPOSITE: *One of the residence's double-height temple-front ends features two terraces, one off the living room and the other off the master suite.*

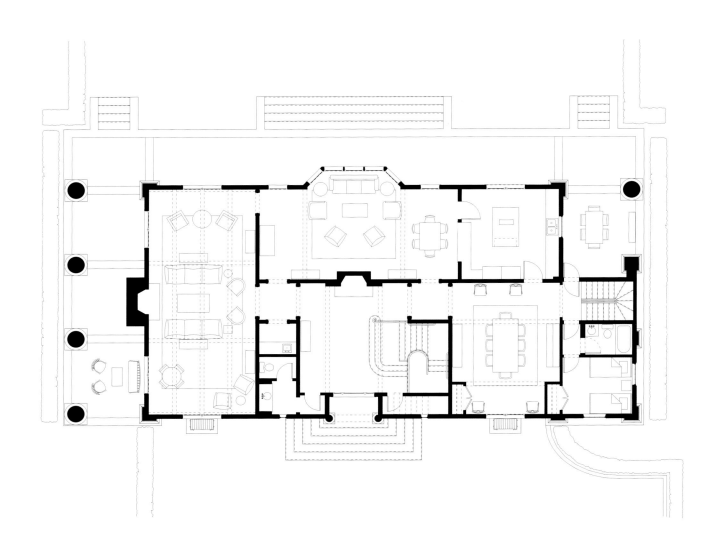

0   5   10   20 ft

ABOVE: *A terrace runs the full length of the house's rear facade.*

LEFT: *The interior design scheme reinforces the Colonial spirit with eighteenth-century antiques, including the family room's drop-leaf desk.*
OPPOSITE: *The dining room features a reissue of Zuber et Cie's 1830s wallpaper "Scenes of North America."*

ABOVE: *An alfresco dining porch faces the garden.*
OPPOSITE: *The second-floor master suite enjoys an
expansive private porch.*

ROCKY MOUNTAIN
RETREAT

Continental Divide, 2005

THE STONE-AND-STUCCO STRUCTURE that sat on this incomparable site near the Continental Divide was unsuited to our client's desire for a contemporary mountain lodge. It featured a low flat roof that partially obscured the views, a poorly organized plan, and an unwanted indoor pool. The lack of a significant front facade also made it difficult to find the front door.

We began by reworking the interior. The pool area became a new family room and a bedroom suite; an additional bedroom was fashioned from an office and adjacent terrace, raising the total from two to four. The flat roofs were replaced with peaked ones, creating shaped ceilings that soar to heights of up to twenty-four feet; these expose the interior to 270-degree vistas and enabled us to insert clerestory windows that bring light into the house's once-dark center.

The ceilings introduced the flavor of a Western lodge, which we reinforced through the material palette. Wyoming Green River stone was selected for the kitchen and baths; walls and fireplaces were finished in a lichen-covered, strongly horizontal Colorado rock; the woods—yew, hemlock, claro walnut—all hail from the Rockies and farther west. Raw nature is expressed in the stonework's exposed fish fossils and the spalted wood veneers used throughout the house. The naturalistic interior proved well suited to the clients' collection of primitive art, and multiple opportunities for display—from open shelving to glass cabinetry—were integrated into the overall design.

The new interior volumes produced a randomly massed exterior with intersecting roof forms, one that nestled organically in its surroundings; to strengthen the connection to nature, we clad the house in rough-edged, undulating stone slabs that echo the strata of a nearby canyon. Interestingly, an important determining factor in the design was a local ordinance: because wood-burning fireplaces were no longer permitted in new construction—and the existing house had eleven—we created the new residence around them, precisely within the original footprint. The sole expansion was an Arts and Crafts–influenced entry portico that establishes the residence's identity and makes the front door unmistakable.

PREVIOUS PAGES: The firm designed an entirely new residence within the footprint of a preexisting house. OPPOSITE: Each room was designed to capture a unique view of the Rocky Mountains.

RIGHT: *The simply massed exterior, with its intersecting roof forms, nestles organically within its surroundings, which emerged almost entirely from an extensive landscaping effort. The house is clad in undulating, rough-edged stone slabs.*

ABOVE: *The preexisting house's low flat roofs were replaced with peaked ones.*
OPPOSITE: *An Arts and Crafts–influenced portico was added to create a formal entry.*

ABOVE AND OPPOSITE: *The owners possessed a collection of primitive objects, figures, and textiles. Multiple opportunities for display—from illuminated glass vitrines to stone shelves jutting from the house's walls and piers—were developed within the design scheme.*

ABOVE: *The new shaped ceilings, introduced throughout the house, open the interior to light and views.* OPPOSITE: *The kitchen's stone countertops feature exposed fish fossils.*

SEASIDE

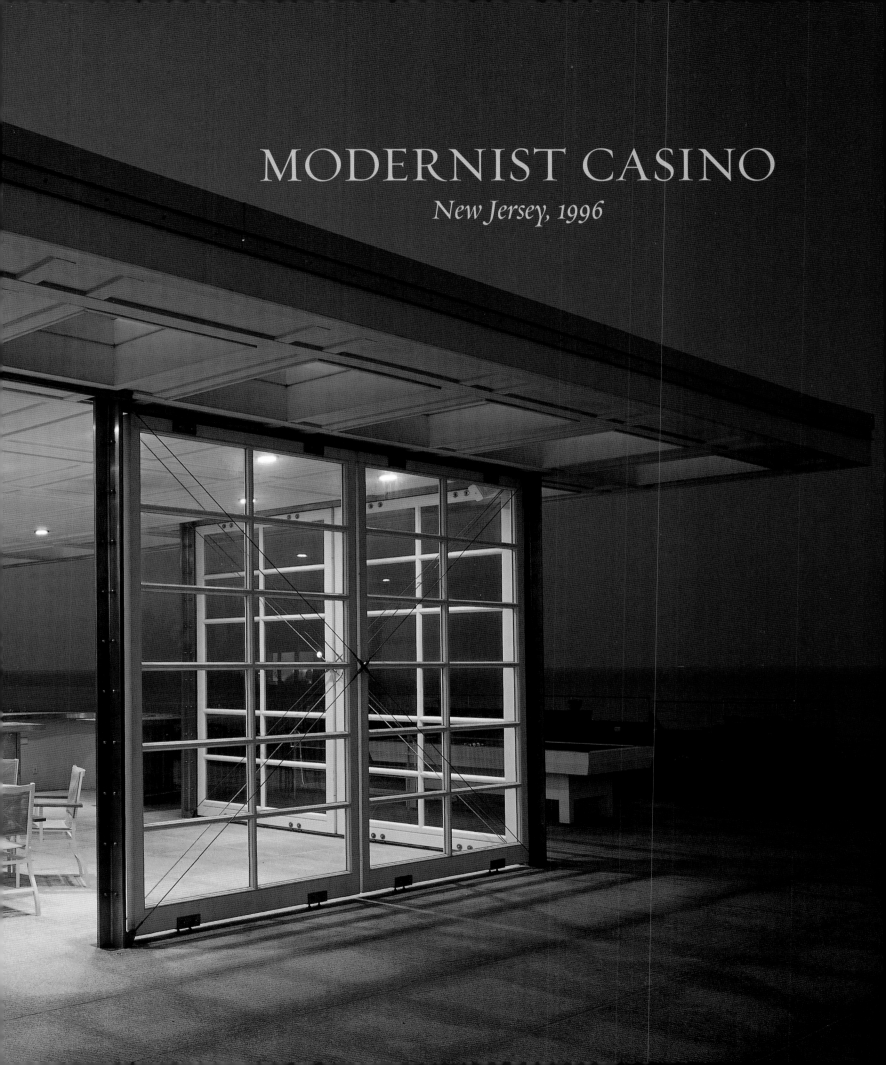

MODERNIST CASINO

New Jersey, 1996

THE LIGHT-HANDED SOUTHERN CALIFORNIA variant of the International Style, developed by Richard Neutra and, later, the Case Study architects in response to that region's gentle climate, provided the model for this simple pool pavilion. Though it is on the New Jersey shore, the structure is paired with a residence that resembles a typical California Contemporary dwelling. And because the client, a retired gentleman, enjoyed sitting beside the sea and playing cards with friends—and thus required little more than elegant protection from the sun and wind—the spare transparency of West Coast modernism provided the ideal solution.

Accordingly, the few elements—a hovering plane supported by cruciform columns and an enclosure for the bath and changing rooms—have been simplified to the greatest possible degree. The breezes arrive only from the southeast, so sliding glazed windbreak panels were installed only at one corner. Square openings along the edges—and a substantial cutout at the center—diminish the presence of the roof.

Paradoxically, a structure this simple, in which every aspect of design and construction remains clearly on display, demands an exceptionally high level of execution. Even small details—for example, arranging the granite pavers so that the columns meet the grid in precisely the right places—received close attention. We also refined the pavilion's simple material palette and hand-fashioned stainless-steel elements from the roof edge and bar to the glides and turnbuckles for the sliding panels. The pristine outcome fully reflects Mies van der Rohe's famous maxim: God is in the details.

PREVIOUS PAGES: *The primary elements of this Modernist pool pavilion—a roof plane and cruciform columns—have been simplified to the greatest possible degree.* OPPOSITE: *Sliding glazed windbreak panels were required only at the southeast corner.*

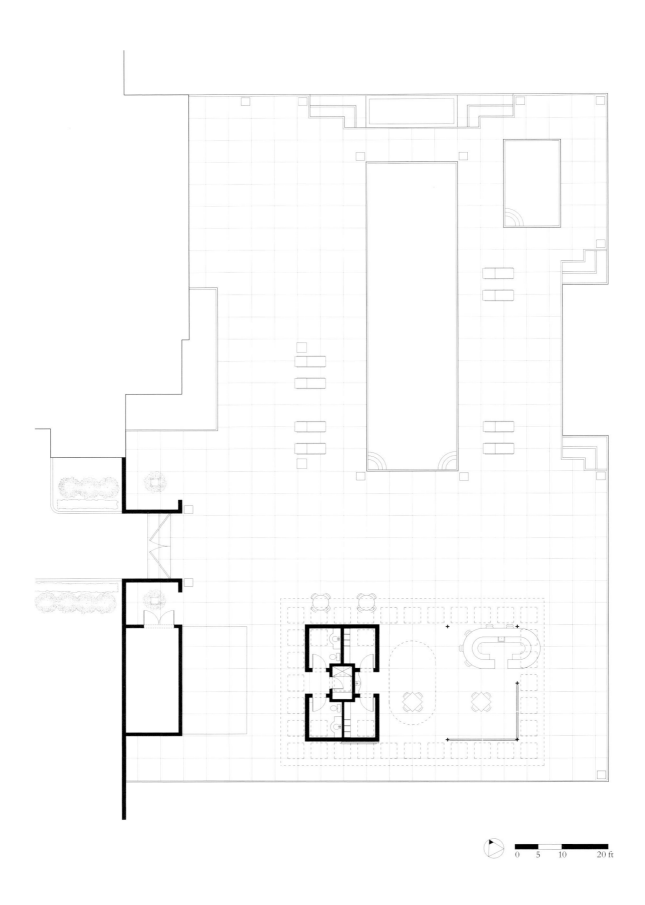

ABOVE: *The pavilion's stainless-steel elements, which include the*
roof edge and bar and the panels' glides and turnbuckles,
were all hand-fashioned. A grid of granite pavers forms the deck.

CLIFFTOP
VILLA

New Jersey, 1999

THE CONCEPT FOR THIS FOUR-BEDROOM summer residence in New Jersey was driven by both local traditions and the singular location. At once constrained and exposed, the site—a rocky perch above the Atlantic—possessed a stark "white cliffs of Dover" beauty that seemed at odds with the symmetrical Italian villa style originally proposed by the client and, indeed, favored by the community. We felt that what was required was a more dynamic, picturesque composition, one that might stake its claim by standing in counterpoint to its setting.

Along with its Mediterranean past, the town also had a strong English architectural history, and the combination called to mind the eighteenth-century English master John Nash. His anglicized Italianate country houses, with their classical yet irregular massing and cooler material and color palettes, are at once restrained and romantic—for our purposes, an ideal combination. Inspired by Nash's 1805 Sandridge Park estate, we developed a balanced asymmetrical design consisting of three different forms: a cylindrical tower, an irregularly shaped central volume, and a large rectilinear block. This combination produced a residence that, from every angle, presents a distinct, different character—a mutable interplay of forms that anchors the house on its site.

Because it was a summer house, we were able to embrace both the out-of-doors and the interior public areas. On the ocean side, all the first-floor rooms adjoin habitable exterior space, and the master suite enjoys two terraces (one for each exposure). This horizontal experience contrasts with the vertical interior view: the double-height entry hall and circulation route, clad in warm white oak, that forms the house's inviting core. While it may seem counterintuitive to give so much weight to stairs and hallways, the upward progression, with its multiple experiential opportunities and views, is as compelling in its changeability as the exterior architecture.

As the oak paneling suggests, material and detail also helped to shape the spatial experience, notably on the main floor. English Gothic plaster moldings define the living and dining areas as discrete rooms even as the cool, continuous Venetian terrazzo floor unites them with the entry hall into a capacious open plan.

PREVIOUS PAGES: *The picturesque, asymmetrical design of this New Jersey summer house, based on an 1805 estate by the English architect John Nash, complements its exposed, oceanside site.*
OPPOSITE: *In contrast to the restrained street front, the house's rear facade is open to the sea at all three levels.*

RIGHT: *A spare classical arcade shades the living room from the morning sun and brings a stately organization to the expansive ocean view.*

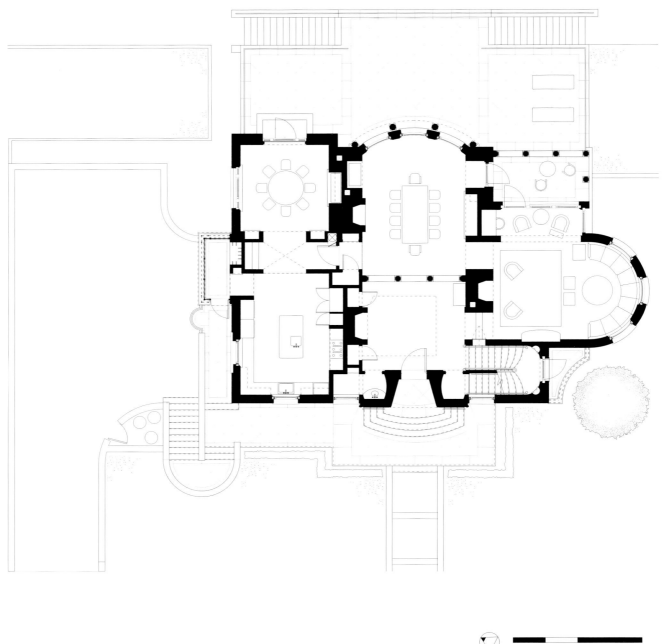

PREVIOUS PAGE: *The double-height entry hall, clad in white oak, celebrates the experience of circulation. Beyond the narrow second-floor screens, built-in seating affords a chance to enjoy the inland vista.*
RIGHT: *The view extends from the front door, through the dining room to the ocean beyond.*

ABOVE: *A series of stone arches lightly screens the dining room from the entry hall. The continuous Venetian terrazzo floor unites the dining area with the living room beyond it, even as the English Gothic moldings articulate the spaces' individuality.* OPPOSITE: *The living room, with its water and shoreline vistas, occupies the lower portion of the house's cylindrical volume. Furniture pieces, including the sideboard and desk, were custom-designed for the space.*

ABOVE: *The cylinder represents the house's most diminutive facade.* OPPOSITE: *The double-height master bath, which occupies the volume's entire upper floor, is extravagantly spacious and airy.*

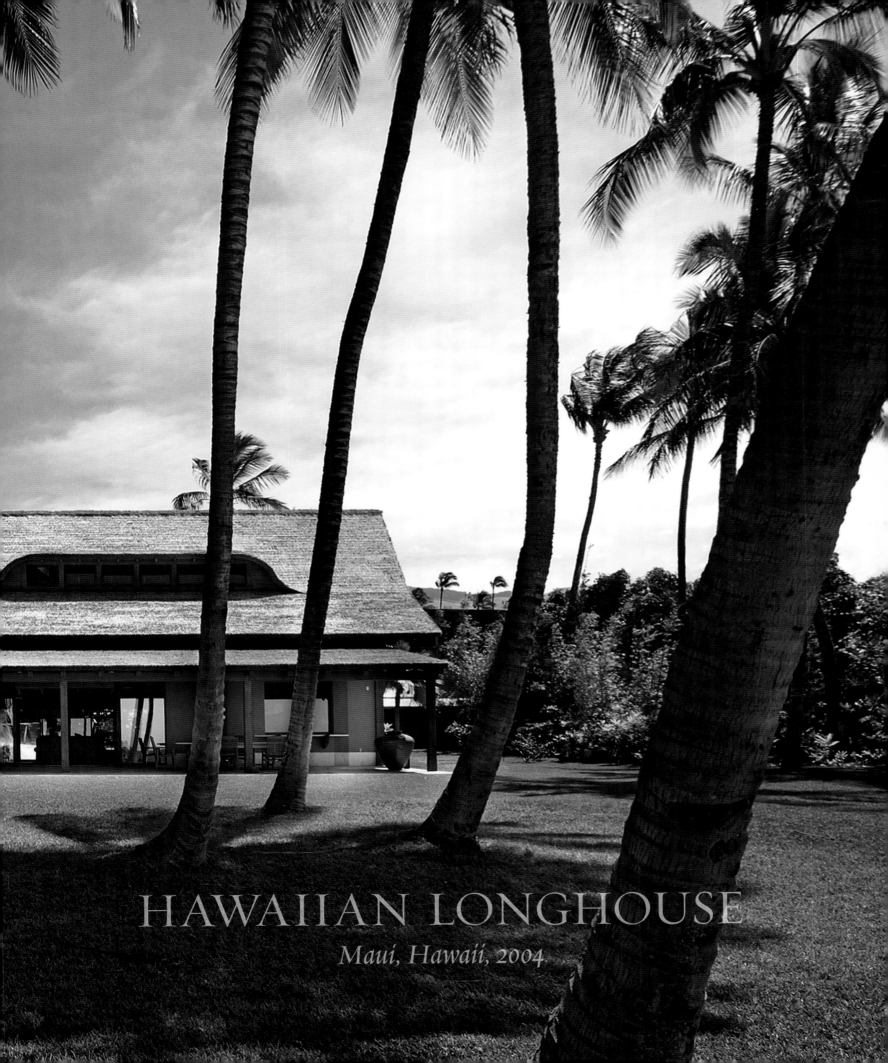

HAWAIIAN LONGHOUSE

Maui, Hawaii, 2004

BECAUSE THIS PROPERTY ADJOINED what our clients described as "the best beach on Maui," they didn't require more from their one-bedroom retreat than that it separate them as minimally as possible from their surroundings. Indeed, the principal request by this Los Angeles–based couple was that the architecture give them a sense of having been transported to an exotic paradise.

That suggested a typology that, sadly, has been all but lost: the vernacular Polynesian longhouse. These linear, semi-enclosed structures were notable for their high, thatch-covered pitched roofs, which drew warm air upward and expelled it through openings near the top, making them ideal for the Hawaiian climate.

Appropriately, the house's centerpiece is a soaring great room, which combines living, kitchen, and informal dining functions. Two thirty-foot-long openings, sited on either side of the space, connect the room to an ocean-facing porch (via a suite of glazed, overscaled pocket doors) and a formal dining area. While the Polynesian influence remains unmistakable, two elements depart notably from the style. In a traditional longhouse, the roof's trusswork was constructed from poles. Here, to create a more tailored interior, a Douglas fir timber frame was crafted in Montana and shipped to the site for installation. We also added long eyebrow dormers—a typical feature of the Shingle Style—to each of the roof slopes. Remote-operated glass panes can be opened to improve ventilation.

Our clients' wish for an elevated master suite, with a balcony from which they could enjoy ocean views, challenged us to introduce a second level into an architectural style that was traditionally a single story. Since the great room is a double-height structure, we were able to integrate a two-story cross piece into the house; its roof pitch, balcony, and visor structure all align with elements of the main volume's roof.

Oriented toward the beach, the bedroom is completely glazed; chamfered corners provide nearly unbroken wraparound views. Glass panels at the edges of the terrace, rather than the usual woven wood railings, ensure that—even from the vantage point of the bed—our clients can experience vistas of the wind-whipped Pacific, surrounding islands, and Hawaiian sunset.

PREVIOUS PAGES: *The firm's design introduced a second floor into part of the traditionally single-story Polynesian longhouse. The eyebrow dormer was borrowed from an unlikely source: the Shingle Style.* OPPOSITE: *The roof's trusswork was constructed from Douglas fir and interspersed with panels of woven bamboo.*

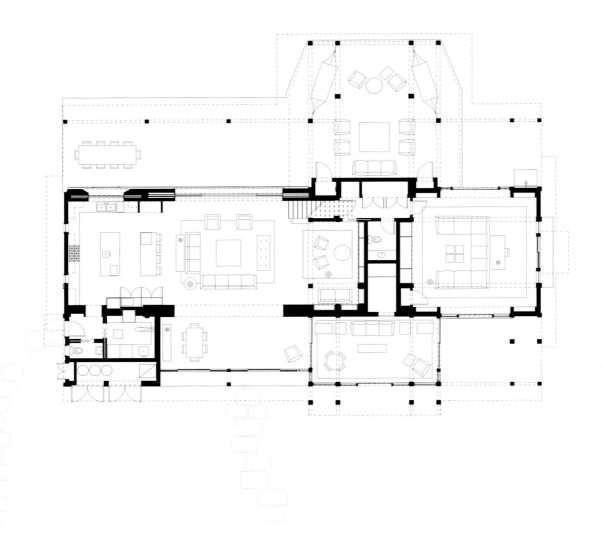

ABOVE: *Much of the house's footprint is actually out-of-doors and shaded from the sun by the thatch-covered pitched roof and its capacious extensions.*

TROPICAL SPLIT-LEVEL

Kaanapali, Hawaii, 2006

THE FIRM'S SCHEME FOR A LUXURIOUS beach bungalow on Maui, situated on a former runway, at once addressed privacy issues posed by close-at-hand neighbors and quandaries posed by our clients' differing aesthetic predilections—she preferred Mediterranean architecture, while he remained partial to the Hawaiian idiom known as "Plantation." We evolved a tripartite design, which answered the husband's interests above, with a Balinese double-pitch roof, and the wife's below, via a stucco podium pierced by arches. In between, we inserted an unlikely yet effective bridge: the early-twentieth-century Craftsman architecture associated with Charles and Henry Greene. This Asian-influenced post-and-beam vocabulary recalled the Pacific Rim tradition of stick shelter, and the Craftsman style's Southern California roots paired as well with the house's Mediterranean elements.

Contending with the site involved creating layers of privacy, which begin upon arrival: the house is set back sixty feet, at the end of a circular drive; a guest cottage shields the drive from the street; and extensive planting masks the adjacent properties, establishing a protected inner court. From here, visitors pass first through a walled garden, then an enclosed lanai, before entering the residence proper. Not until the living room does the experience open outward again—toward a panoramic yet carefully screened ocean view.

To capture that view, we elevated the living room to a height of six feet, which produced a split-level structure: the playroom and pool are at ground level, below the main floor, and the bedrooms rise a half-level above the living room. While the vista is maximized by a series of pocket doors that open the house to the ocean-facing lanai, the design also establishes an alternative, interior view via a series of communicating, vaulted public spaces. These flow into the residence's two-story private wing, which is crowned by the master suite.

Against a light-colored plaster backdrop, Craftsman-inspired layers of detail were applied with a selection of woods whose tones and textures enabled us to differentiate between the residence's various elements. Red cedar and afromosia appear on the exterior; floors and kitchen cabinetry are built from teak; and such decorative elements as diffuser grilles and balusters employ indigenous koa wood.

PREVIOUS PAGES: *The design of this house unites a Balinese double-pitch roof and a Mediterranean-style podium.* OPPOSITE: *A terrace reveals part of the extensive selection of woods with which the house was detailed.*

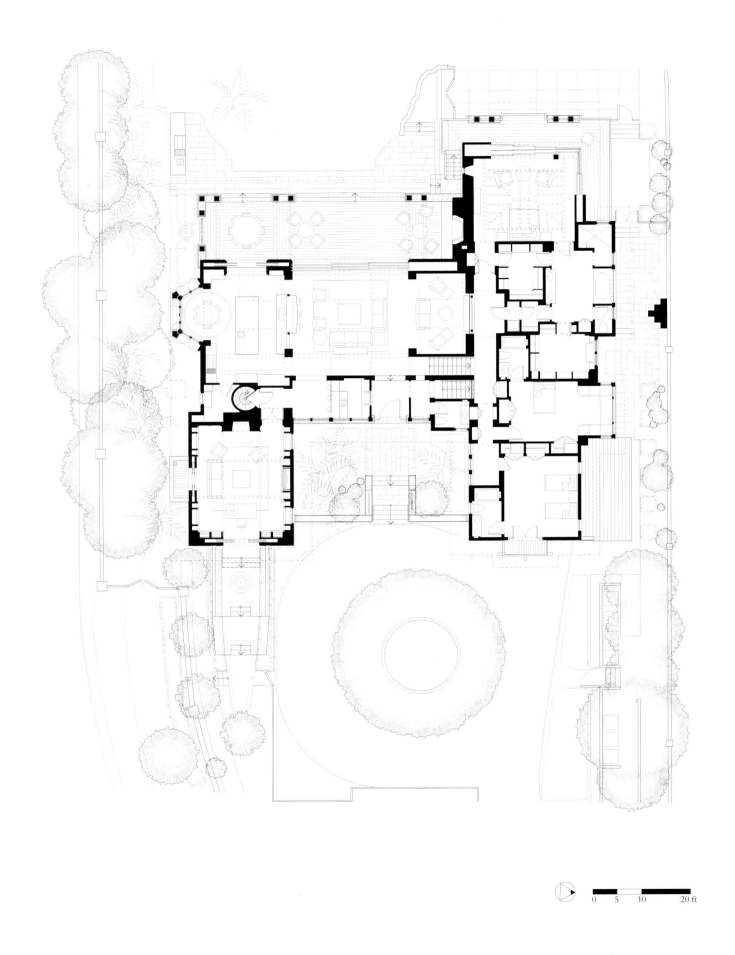

0   5   10   20 ft

ABOVE: *To ensure privacy, the house is set back sixty feet from the road, at the edge of a circular drive. A walled garden and an enclosed lanai precede the main entrance.*

ABOVE: *To capture the ocean view, the living room was elevated to a height of six feet. The playroom and pool remain at ground level.*
OPPOSITE: *The lawn, the product of massive infill on what was once a perfectly flat airport runway, floats between the two levels.*

SHINGLE STYLE
BEACH HOUSE

Eastern Long Island, 2000

ON AN EXPANSIVE PROPERTY overlooking Moriches Bay on Long Island's eastern end, our client chose to fulfill a longstanding dream: to build a grand and iconic Shingle Style residence for himself, his wife, and their three young daughters. Encouraged to hold nothing back, we turned to a work that amounts to a Bible of the style at its zenith: George Sheldon's 1887 classic *Artistic Country-Seats*. In its pages, we found magnificent houses by great practitioners—H. H. Richardson, Wilson Eyre, Bruce Price, and McKim, Mead & White— and used them as the well from which to draw inspiration for our client's fantasia.

It was not difficult to find historical quotations suitable to the program—which, not surprisingly, included multiple classic Shingle Style features, among them deep porches, window bays, and a tower. The challenge instead lay in combining these elements into a resolved composition. The stylistic origins are unmistakable, yet the outcome is original, specific, and responsive to both the lessons of twentieth-century architecture and the preferences of contemporary living.

The essential design follows the historic convention of a long bar with various elements pulled forward to different degrees, producing an asymmetrical composition of symmetrical parts. (A second wing, containing the garages, extends perpendicular from the main house.) At the same time, the emphasis remains on motifs that subtly move the architecture into the present, such as the elimination of decorative trim, which produces the taut, organic quality of the shingle wrapper. Within, the rooms reflect vernacular Shingle Style design, but we dispensed with the custom of entering into a great hall that serves as the principal public space. Instead, the plan reduced the house in most places to the thickness of a single room—which promotes cross ventilation, balanced light, and multiple views—and wherever possible, rooms lead from one to the next, thereby eliminating hallways.

Similarly, the design of the interior carefully intersperses historical precedents—Stanford White's own home is quoted in the matchstick-bamboo-over-red-paint frieze in the living room—with moments of modernity. A notable instance appears in the kitchen: exploring a nautical theme, which included a maple-and-teak, decklike floor and the white-painted wood and mahogany characteristic of yacht design, we added riveted, painted-steel backsplash panels.

PREVIOUS PAGES: *This Shingle Style beach house consists of a long volume with various elements pulled forward to different degrees.* OPPOSITE: *Symmetrical moments recur in the house's larger asymmetrical composition.*

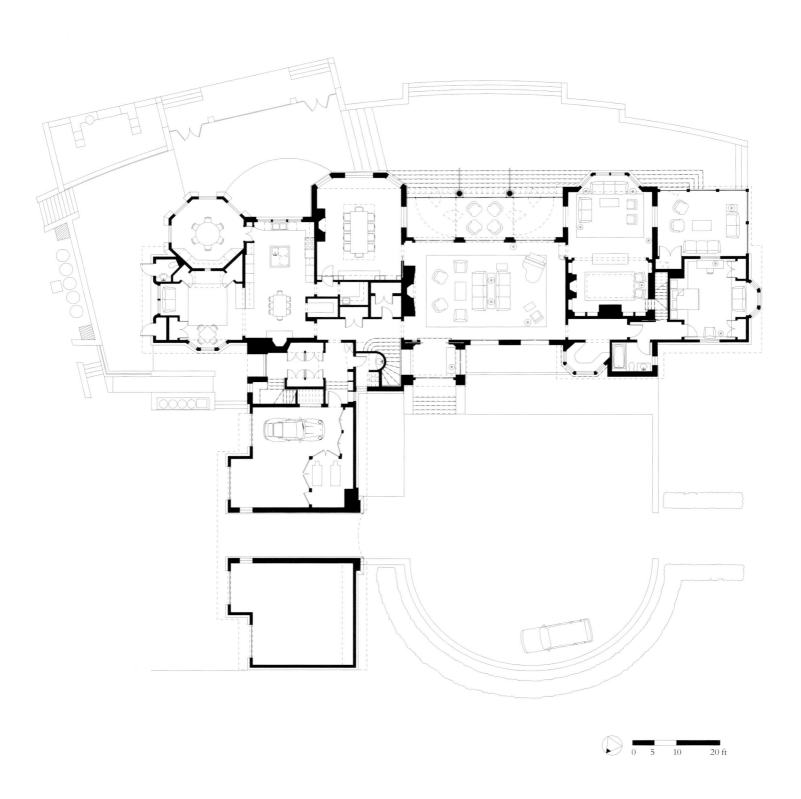

ABOVE: *The view from the entry vestibule passes through a lattice portal to a circular stair landing.* OPPOSITE: *The suspended gallery of the double-story library—hung from nautical chains—features a teak lattice walkway, which brings light into the space below.*

BEACH RETREAT
Cabo San Lucas, Mexico, 2009

ALTHOUGH THE FIRM HAD A FREE HAND on the ocean-facing side of this beachfront property near Cabo San Lucas, a different mandate prevailed on the street: local architectural guidelines required that, however large, new homes resemble the multiple small dwellings found in a typical Mexican village. Our solution produced what might be called a house divided: to the street it offers the multipane windows, peaked tile roofs, and close-set volumes associated with regional vernacular architecture; to the ocean it presents the sweeping curves and glass expanses of a contemporary villa.

The design was also influenced by the tightly constrained site, with large residences on adjacent lots. Our clients wanted privacy and a protected lawn on which their young children could play. So rather than curving the house outward toward the Pacific, which would have exposed its side windows to the neighbors and consumed habitable landscape, we reversed the curve to create a concave oceanside elevation. Not only did this provide views to all the water-facing rooms while shielding them from prying eyes, it facilitated the creation of a protected, lozenge-shaped lawn, some thirty-five feet at its deepest. Beyond this, a convex negative-edge pool completes the property. The resulting procession—from the living room to a pergola-covered terrace to the lawn, the pool, and the incomparable sea view—unites the natural and man-made into a single experience.

While a village-like complexity was imposed in front, the interior is complex by choice: we sought to enliven it with a wide variety of experiences. An open floor plan distinguishes the public rooms, which look outward across the lawn and pool toward the ocean. The intimately scaled master suite, by contrast, has a private walled garden with an outdoor fireplace and its own pool. A guest room enjoys views on all four sides. The three children's suites overlook an entirely different vista.

Influenced by the location's physical drama and Mexico's artistic heritage, the design engages at every opportunity with color, bold forms, and the elements. Two moments capture this with particular force. One is the fire pit, which rises from the center of a circular pool set just above the beach. The other is the cobalt blue, Pantheon-like grotto adjacent to the media room—with an oculus at its peak, it remains open to the sun, wind, and weather.

PREVIOUS PAGES: *The negative-edge pool curves around the entire oceanside perimeter of this Mexican villa.*
OPPOSITE: *The front door opens onto a direct view to the ocean.*

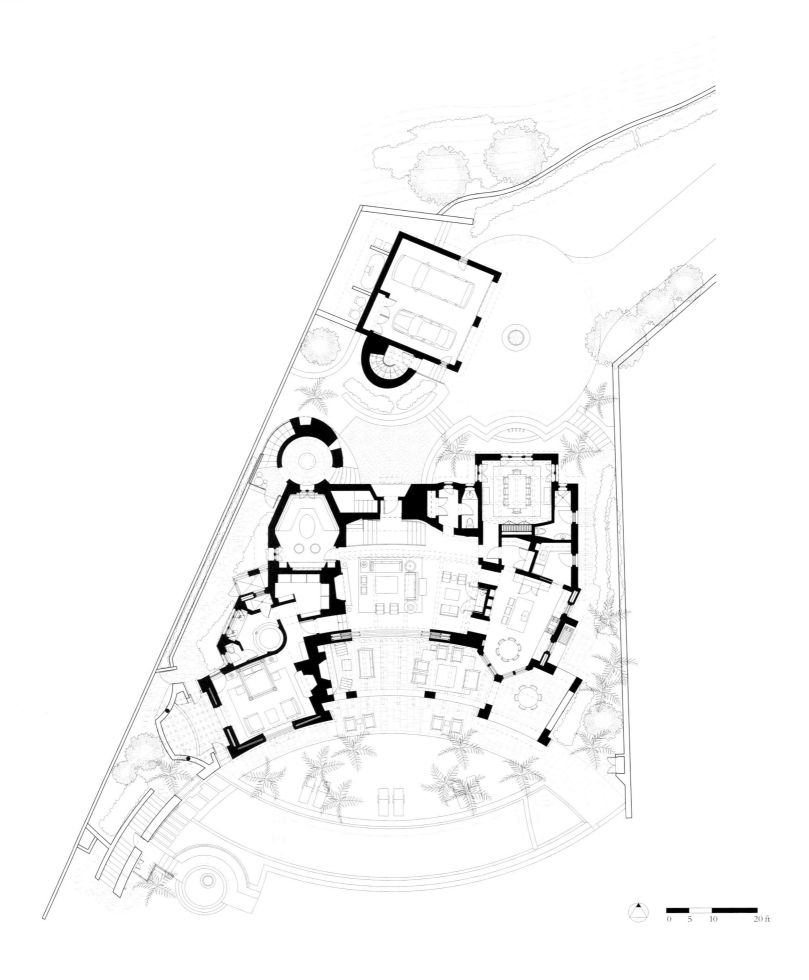

ABOVE: *The house offers to the street the design*
elements of traditional village architecture.

LEFT: *The Pantheon-like grotto features an open oculus; when it rains, water streams in and is collected in a cistern directly beneath.*
OPPOSITE: *The use of strong colors—a Mexican aesthetic tradition—reinforces the house's bold and simple architectural forms.*

RIGHT: *The rough-hewn palo de arco ceiling of the pergola continues into the living room, uniting interior and exterior. The change of elevation in the house's sloping site is reflected in the course of the stair.*

ABOVE: *Cobalt blue niches in the kitchen represent a contemporary interpretation of a Mexican tradition.* OPPOSITE: *The open living room doors frame a view across the pergola and the lawn to the pool, which seems to dissolve into the ocean.*

ABOVE: *The house's rear facade brings together a series of gracefully intersecting curvilinear forms.* OPPOSITE: *On the pergola, a thick wall—another local architectural tradition—creates the opportunity for dual columns of decorative niches.*

NORMAN HOUSE
ON THE SOUND

Greenwich, Connecticut, 2004

THIS CONNECTICUT PROPERTY, which slopes down to Long Island Sound, posed an atypical condition: it measured eight hundred feet in length but only one hundred feet in width, compelling us to dramatically compress what would ordinarily have been a volume elongated to capitalize on the view. Our clients' fondness for French medieval architecture, specifically the Cistercian abbeys of Burgundy, provided the solution. We conceived of a residence that might seem, like many medieval buildings, to be a fragment of something larger. The unusually narrow stone structure has stucco sides, which make it seem as though the entire mass had been sliced from the center of a bread loaf.

Though the design strategy began in Burgundy, it moved west to embrace elements of the Norman style. This influence is most apparent in the first-floor great room, an unbroken span of seventy-five feet—the house's full interior width—loosely divided into library, living, and family areas. We were also inspired by the instances, often found in historic structures, in which fragments from different periods collide to unexpectedly poetic effect. In the dining room, which occupies the lower floor of a two-story central bay window, we stopped the vaulted ceiling six feet before it reached the glazed exterior wall. This created a double-height space, overlooked from above by the enclosed master suite: a mysterious architectural quirk suggestive of a structure that had evolved—not always logically—over time.

The project also enabled the firm to explore material and craft, evident immediately upon arrival in both the entry ceiling, constructed of reclaimed oak and elm, and the joinery securing the ironwork balustrades to the balcony's jigsawed support beams. For the exterior, Pennsylvania stone was selected for its rough-hewn quality; within, varieties of whiter, fine-grained French limestone, milled to a smooth finish, lend authority to the floors and walls.

One of the most unexpected features—the pond that fills the entire forecourt—was suggested by our client. The initial design, a circle within a square, gave way at his suggestion to a more organically shaped waterscape, interspersed with native plantings, stocked with koi, and bridged by zigzagging slabs of bluestone. Rather than being at odds with our medieval mélange, this Asian-style water garden seems—like the residence itself—to be part of the long, varied history of the site.

OPPOSITE: *An organically shaped waterscape fills the forecourt of this Connecticut residence.*

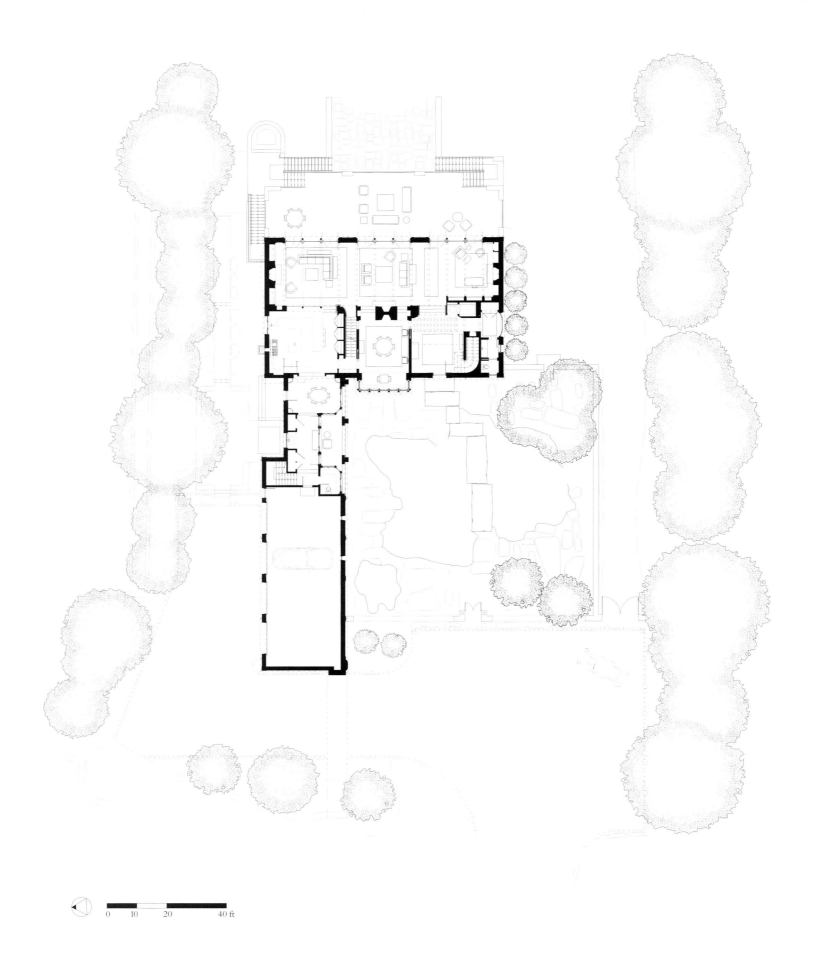

0   10   20   40 ft

ABOVE: *The house's French medieval style, which evolved from the clients' fondness for the Cistercian abbeys of Burgundy, suited the long but narrow waterfront site.*

RIGHT: *A Norman influence is most evident in the first floor's great room, which provides areas for library, living room, and family room.*

LEFT: *The stuccoed side elevations suggest that the residence is an architectural fragment of a once-larger structure.* OPPOSITE: *A strong commitment to materiality and craft is evident in the entry ceiling, constructed from reclaimed oak and elm.*

ABOVE: *Both the entry hall and dining room are visible from the great room.*
OPPOSITE: *The residence's lower level encloses an indoor swimming pool.*

ABOVE AND OPPOSITE: *From every point, the master suite enjoys incomparable views of Long Island Sound.*

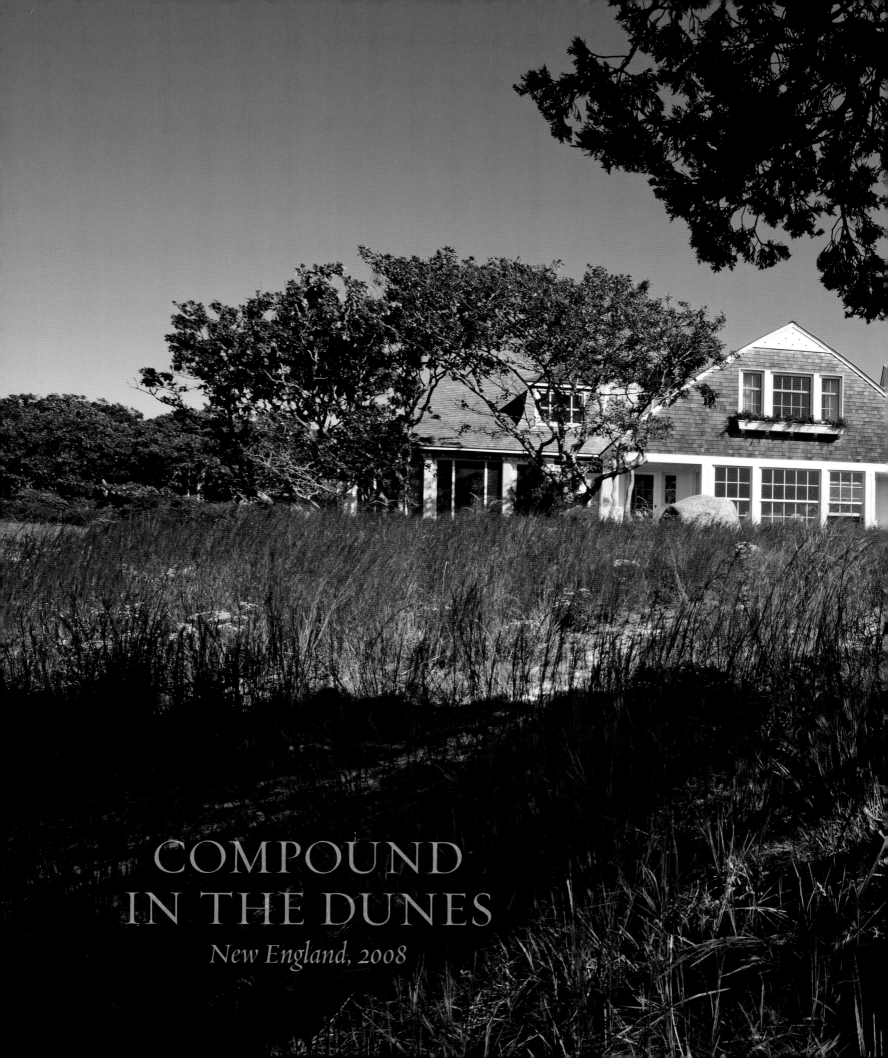

COMPOUND
IN THE DUNES

New England, 2008

OUR CONCEPT FOR A BEACH HOUSE on a rolling site overlooking the Atlantic Ocean brings together two seemingly contrasting ideas—nineteenth-century Shingle Style design and a contemporary preference for material and textural expression over architectural detail—both of which were favored by our clients. While the exterior captures the local design aesthetic, the interior treats light, space, and surface in a distinctly modern fashion. Throughout, suggestions of each approach inform, and strengthen, the other.

The structure is considerably larger than a classic Cape Cod residence, but also proportionally thinner than its historic predecessors. The result is a home that sits lightly on the land, its porosity enhanced by a broad breezeway and deep porches. A bowed gable—a traditional feature of vernacular craftwork that recalls the upside-down hull of a ship—appears on the oceanside facade. Its curvilinear form reappears in other exterior elements: a concave shed dormer that seems to melt into the roof, chimneys that slope and tilt inward, columns that flare at the top.

Inside, the typical building blocks of a New England beach house—unfinished flooring, painted wooden boards, and white-washed brick—are deployed unexpectedly, in the service of a clean-lined, open-plan design. A white-painted entry hall, with a wall of windows revealing a courtyard view, serves as a gallery that flows from the study past the living room to the stairwell and family room beyond. In the living room, ten-foot-high, triple-hung windows—inspired by the Louisiana architecture of A. Hays Town—open to nearly seven feet, dissolving the distinction between interior and exterior. These interconnecting, light-filled rooms are contrasted with a series of discrete cocoonlike spaces, finished in such warm materials as cork and oak and further enriched by fireplaces.

Three outbuildings also partake in the dialogue between present and past. A three-bedroom guest cottage replicates the balance of tradition and modernity evident in the main house. A barn pairs an eighteenth-century frame discovered in Maine with antique hemlock siding. And the pool house is design-forward in its mix of elements, encasing a glass-and-steel volume in teak louvers. In a bit of postmodern irony, its cedar-shingled roof precisely mirrors the pitch of the one atop the main house.

PREVIOUS PAGES: *A traditional bowed gable appears on the ocean front of this beach house.* OPPOSITE: *A light-filled entry gallery connects the major public rooms.*

ABOVE AND OPPOSITE: *A prominent breezeway and generous porches enhance the lightness with which the house occupies its site.* OVERLEAF: *Ten-foot-high triple-hung windows dominate the living room wall.*

ABOVE AND OPPOSITE: *While the interior features the typical materials of a beach house, including simple wood floors and painted boards and brick, the design takes a nontraditional approach to light, space, and surface.*

ABOVE: *An organic, flitch-sawn headboard in the master suite recalls the work of George Nakashima.* OPPOSITE: *The back stair, enclosed in a lozenge-shaped tube lined with vertical boards, draws illumination from a light monitor at the top.*

ABOVE AND OPPOSITE: *The barn, one of three outbuildings on the property, pairs an eighteenth-century frame found in Maine with antique hemlock siding.*

ABOVE AND OPPOSITE: *While the primary residence balances traditional and contemporary elements, the pool house—which encloses a glass and steel volume in teak louvers—is a firmly modern work of architecture.*

VILLA ON THE
ATLANTIC

New Jersey, 2004

THE GREAT ITALIAN ARCHITECT Carlo Scarpa remains particularly admired for the museum projects he completed in his country's Veneto region. Into a series of medieval buildings, Scarpa inserted modern interventions that, rather than seeming out of place, established a rich, complex interplay between the present and the past.

We thought of Scarpa's approach when the firm was engaged to design a seven-bedroom beach house for a generous-spirited client, one whose enthusiasm for Mediterranean architecture was equaled by his fondness for entertaining. First, we conceived of an Italianate structure with an H-shaped plan—two wings joined by a slender volume—reminiscent of Andrea Palladio's Villa Trissino. Then, having produced a "historic" work, we shifted into Scarpa mode: rather than constructing the central volume from masonry, we designed a twenty-two-by-forty-five-foot living/dining hall shaped by two modern curtain walls of stainless steel and glass. As the room's heavily beamed ceiling and limestone floors flow outward to front and back loggias, visitors receive an impression of a sixteenth-century open-air court that has been enclosed by a contemporary renovation. Moreover, the fourteen-foot-high ceiling, twin fireplaces, and simple, strong furnishings make it an ideal gathering place, one that encourages easy passage between interior and exterior—the flavor being not unlike that of an elegant seaside resort.

This grand apportioning of space carries over into the master suite, which is directly above the living/dining room and enjoys the same ceiling height and footprint. Secondary areas—inglenook, kitchenette, and closets—are screened off by eight-foot-high wood walls inserted at either end of the main room. This provides separation between the spaces without fully enclosing them. Two other wings house the remaining bedrooms, an office, the kitchen, and various social areas, including a family room and a bar. All receive ocean or inland views.

Among the house's most striking aspects is its carefully staged arrival sequence: a four hundred-foot-long drive passes a sunken tennis court, concealed from initial view by a hedge, and ends at an imposing flight of steps that spans the full width of the front loggia. At its apex, visitors are greeted not by the anticipated grand entrance but by the curtain wall, which frames an expansive vista of the lawns and, beyond them, the Atlantic.

PREVIOUS PAGES: *The volumes of this oceanside villa, at the end of a four hundred-foot-long drive, were inspired by Andrea Palladio's Villa Trissino.* OPPOSITE: *The Italian artist Mario Ceroli created the circular table in the main hall.*

RIGHT: *The insertion of a glazed living room volume within the masonry loggia at once promotes transparency through the house and encourages easy passage between interior and exterior.*
OVERLEAF: *Carlo Scarpa's influence is evident in the mantelpiece of the living/dining hall. The custom-designed chandeliers marry the medieval and the modern.*

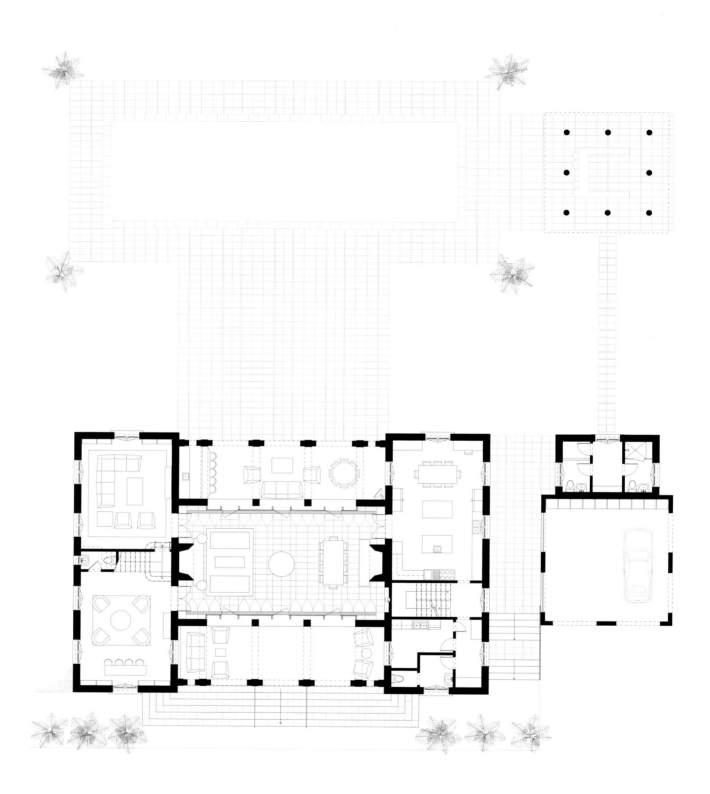

0 5 10   20 ft

CITYSIDE

MODERN
DUPLEX
New York, New York, 2006

THIS FIVE-BEDROOM DUPLEX, in a classic postwar building on Manhattan's Upper East Side, suffered from certain of the liabilities particular to the period, such as low ceiling heights. Yet it also benefited from many assets, in particular northern and southern exposures finished almost entirely in glass. Asked to design a home for a family with four children, we chose to embrace the stylistic context, reinforcing and expanding upon the space's midcentury modern roots.

On the apartment's first, public floor, we removed almost all of the walls to produce a spacious loftlike environment that opens the interior to the superlative light and views. Gridlike patterns, inspired by the twentieth-century Italian design polymath Gio Ponti, enliven the solid "bookend" walls to the east and west. Combined with the open plan, the simple organizational strategy facilitates visual connection and orientation across the entire first floor.

The focal point of the design is the staircase, which we enclosed in softly lit glass panels. Formerly a Sheetrock-clad obstruction, the "stair cube" now reads as the glowing hub from which all the surrounding areas radiate. On the second, private floor, which contains four children's bedrooms and a master suite, this transparency is, by necessity, reversed.

The interior design program continues the architecture's midcentury emphasis. Acting as curators, we selected pieces by, among others, Ponti, Eliel Saarinen, Serge Mouille, Alvar Aalto, and Finn Juhl; a collection of colorful Orrefors objects adorns the custom-designed glass display system in the study. Unusual grid-patterned rugs inspired by the postwar Swedish textile designer Barbro Nilsson subtly complete the urbane design scheme.

PREVIOUS PAGES: *The firm removed almost all the walls on the first floor of this midcentury modern duplex.* OPPOSITE: *In the entry, a grid-patterned rug, its design influenced by the Swedish textile designer Barbro Nilsson, reinforces the design scheme.*

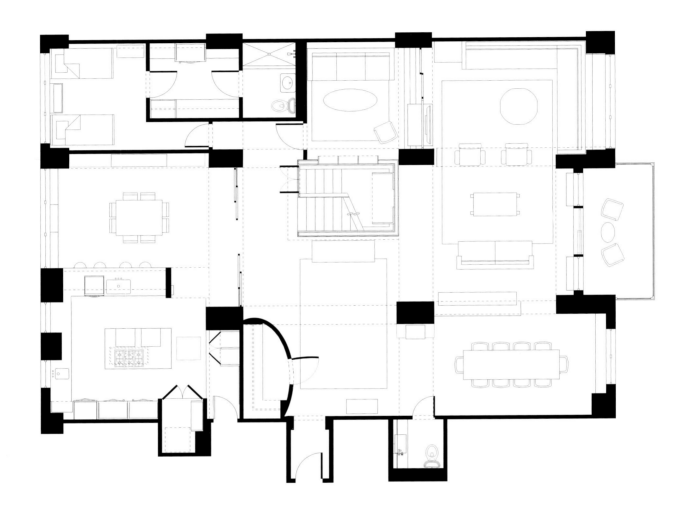

0   5   10   20 ft

ABOVE: *Custom-designed glass shelves in the study are backlit by the glass-enclosed "stair cube."*

RIGHT: *Gridlike patterns, inspired by the twentieth-century designer Gio Ponti, embellish solid walls on the first floor. The vintage furniture was designed by Saarinen, Mouille, Aalto, and Juhl, among others.*

RIGHT: *Positioned behind the entry, the kitchen at once participates in and stands apart from the first floor's open plan.*

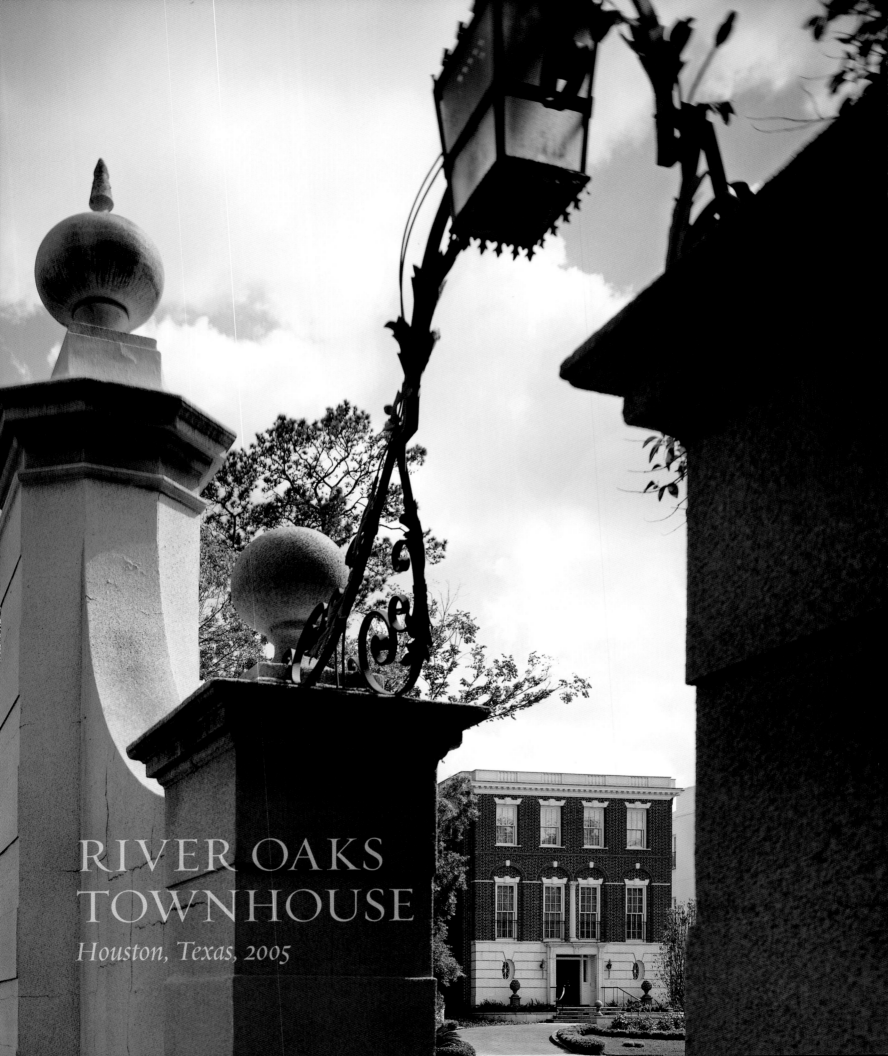

RIVER OAKS
TOWNHOUSE

Houston, Texas, 2005

AFTER LIVING FOR DECADES in a Georgian mansion in the heart of Houston's suburban River Oaks district, our clients decided to reinvent their life in a new form and context. Purchasing a smaller lot on the area's more urban edge, they commissioned a townhouse that would incorporate a selection of architectural and design objects from their old home, which the new owners had decided to demolish.

Because our clients had requested a brick Georgian residence, we took as a template the 1809 townhouse of Charleston, South Carolina, merchant Nathaniel Russell. From there, we developed a dialogue between the couple's previous experience of suburban gentility—as embodied by a rambling house rooted in a single style—and their new life and interests. These involved not only embracing a more modern diversity of aesthetic influences but also creating a showcase for their previously undisplayed artworks. Their remarkable collection included twentieth-century Latin American and Eastern European paintings, notably an important selection of pictures by female Surrealists.

The meeting of past and present begins at the front door. Entering through the limestone portal that framed the previous house's entry, visitors discover a Wiener Werkstätte–inspired reception hall that stands in striking contrast to the exterior. We extended this influence upward via an elliptical Art Deco ironwork stair, developed from a sketch our client made of an architectural detail in Berlin. This forms a Moderne spine linking the two Federal-style floors above.

At the same time, details large and small drawn from the old house—from door surrounds, moldings, and windows to knobs and hinges—were woven into the architectural fabric of the rooms. An even earlier layer of memory and history appears in the master bedroom: the design of the vaulted ceiling was taken from the residence of our client's grandfather, an oilman whose mansion, designed by John F. Staub, was one of the architectural highlights of 1930s Houston.

While the outcome is, at every scale, a uniquely personal residence, designing a new structure around preexisting elements created complex challenges. The largest of these is hinted at by two unusually close-set windows, united by a column into a Florentine motif, in the middle of the facade. This seemingly decorative flourish in fact corrects an asymmetry caused by a lack of correspondence between the first- and second-floor axes—one imposed by the need to set the old entry portal in the center.

PREVIOUS PAGES: *The townhouse design was inspired by an 1809 Charleston, South Carolina, residence.* OPPOSITE: *The ground-floor entry hall was influenced by the Wiener Werkstätte.*

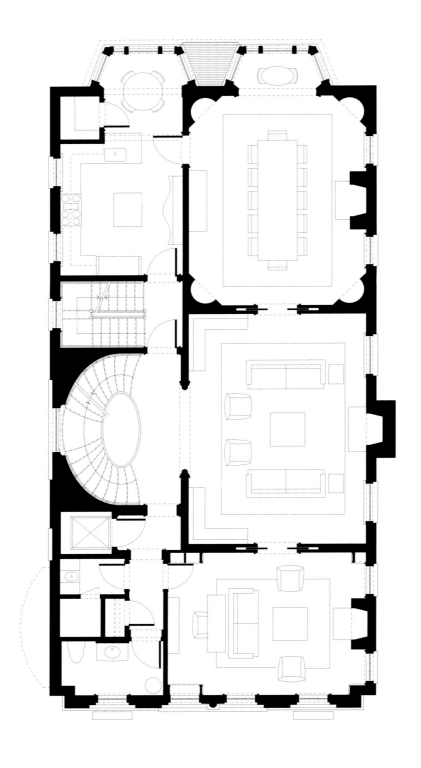

PREVIOUS PAGE: *An elliptical stair is a Moderne spine linking the second and third floors.*
RIGHT: *The living room serves as a showcase for a collection of twentieth-century artworks.*

ABOVE: *The house features architectural and design elements from the clients' previous home, including moldings and door surrounds.*
OPPOSITE: *The Escher-like floor adds a modern accent to the kitchen.*

LOFT
IN TRIBECA
New York, New York, 2000

WHEN OUR CLIENTS, A COUPLE with a young daughter, purchased this loft in a former warehouse in Manhattan's Tribeca district, it was a fifty-by-eighty-foot box evincing traditional details—steel beams, cast-iron columns, an exposed-joist ceiling—and a subsequently added foot-deep concrete floor. The brief was simple: to introduce the necessary program without sacrificing the drama delivered by eighty unbroken feet and—because the main windows were situated at either end of that span—to bring light into the loft's dark heart.

As believers in contextualism, we often take aesthetic cues from the vernacular styles surrounding a project. In Tribeca, the architectural context is both industrial and modern; combined with the need to break out of the grid imposed by the space's columns, this led us to an interplay of free-floating, overlapping horizontal and vertical planes.

To raise the ceiling height from ten to eleven feet, we removed the concrete floor, except at the entry, so as to avoid having to recalibrate the elevator (which opens directly into the residence); the resulting runwaylike platform, hovering a foot above the main space, affords an introductory view down the loft's full length and launches the planar design scheme. The need to conceal pipes belonging to the upstairs residence produced a "white zone" spanning the loft's kitchen and midsection beneath a floating plane that, with its random constellation of downlights, illuminates the loft's once-gloomy center.

Siting rooms along the loft's periphery maintained the long central span; sliding panels in the kitchen and study preserve a connection between these spaces and the adjoining public areas. And though the need for a home office made it impossible to keep the loft completely open from end to end, the office's principal wall, constructed of squares and rectangles of translucent acrylic, glows with daylight from north-facing windows.

To break out of the columnar grid, we allowed spaces to slip into one another. The living room's wall of custom-designed zinc bookshelves flows into the private study. The upper part of the office wall pushes into the master suite, where it becomes a soffit above the bed. And to move the living room beyond the tight sixteen-by-sixteen-foot square enforced by an existing column, we designed a twenty-two-by-twenty-two-foot felt rug with an egg-shaped hole and grid-line zippers to accommodate the immovable structure.

PREVIOUS PAGES: *In the living room of a Tribeca loft, a wall of custom-designed bookshelves serves as a de facto art piece.*
OPPOSITE: *A Mondrian-inspired translucent wall encloses the study.*

RIGHT: *A "white zone" in the middle of the loft conceals pipes and introduces illumination.*

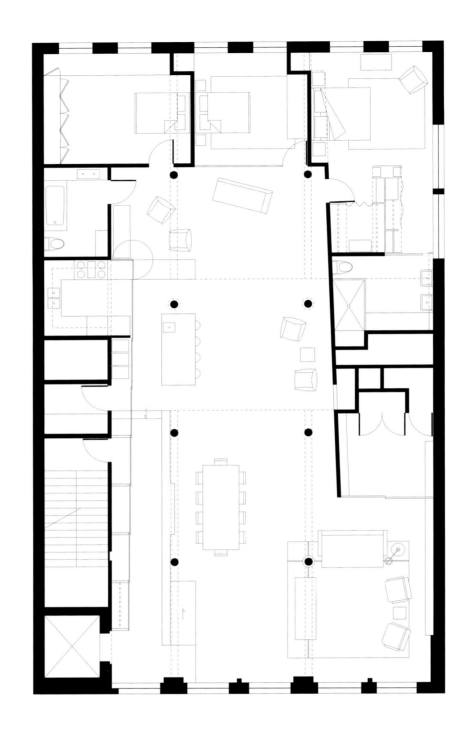

0   5   10   20 ft

ABOVE: *A zenlike calm characterizes the master bedroom.*

WEDGE LOFT

New York, New York, 2000

EMERGING FROM THE ELEVATOR directly into this top-floor Manhattan loft, we encountered a surprising, singular space: a ninety-foot-long, three-dimensional wedge that expanded from twelve to fifty feet in width and swept dramatically upward, culminating in a twenty-four-foot-high, south-facing wall of glass. The design challenge lay in preserving the drama of this spatial explosion while adding the functions necessary to convert what had been an industrial loft into a two-bedroom residence.

The firm's solution was a forty-foot-long suite of freestanding cabinets that ran parallel to the eastern, angled wall and separated the major private spaces from the capacious public area. This strategy enabled the program to migrate naturally into several different zones: the living/kitchen/dining functions filled the principal space; the master bath and dressing area were tucked behind the cabinet wall. The study was sited behind the elevator in the loft's narrow end, along with a stair that ascended to a small, second-floor guest suite.

The main bedroom was set in a transitional space, between the living room and master bath and dressing areas; instead of a conventional enclosure, we created a semicircle from three translucent panels set in steel frames. Inspired by the industrial/mechanical aesthetic of the twentieth-century French architect Pierre Chareau, this fanlike construction can be pulled open or closed based on the owner's need for privacy.

Given that the loft's original condition was at once industrial and—as the Tuscan columns and Douglas fir floor suggest—handcrafted, the residence was detailed from both perspectives. Like the master bedroom enclosure, the red-painted steel stair owes a debt to Chareau; the cabinets were covered in a resin-coated linen normally used to make circuit boards; and the master bath is finished in a hexagonal ceramic tile associated with New York's older residential buildings. By contrast, the ceiling is paneled in a warm oak evocative of the columns and floor. And as a sculptural collage crafted from steel plate, the fireplace—which combines a wood-burning stove and, in place of a hearth, a television—expresses both sensibilities.

PREVIOUS PAGES AND OPPOSITE: *Both the semicircle of translucent panels that conceal the master bedroom and the red-painted steel stair were inspired by French architect Pierre Chareau.*

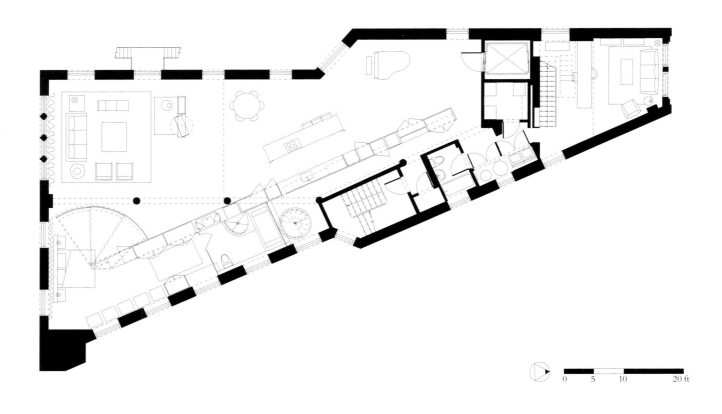

ABOVE: *The panels enclosing the master bedroom slide open or closed.*
RIGHT: *Freestanding cabinets parallel the eastern wall of the loft.*

ANTIQUARIAN'S
APARTMENT

San Francisco, California, 2008

THE DESIGN DIRECTION FOR THIS San Francisco apartment, created for an antiques dealer with a collection of eighteenth-century French and Italian furniture, derived from two powerful factors. The first was its exclusive location at the top of Nob Hill, directly across the street from Grace Cathedral, the storied Pacific-Union Club, and Huntington Park. The second factor was the building's equally exclusive pedigree: its original interiors had been created by the path-breaking twentieth-century decorator Elsie de Wolfe. We combined the interests and personality of our Eurocentric client with the spirit of de Wolfe's aesthetic, which—like San Francisco itself—mixed Western exuberance with Continental elegance. The outcome suggests an opulent eighteenth-century French residence redone by a great American decorator.

The firm's initial efforts focused on reorganizing the rooms to maximize their dramatic impact. The master suite, which adjoined the living room and faced the street, was relocated to a more secluded zone, and the space converted to a library. This produced a T-shaped plan in which visitors enter a long gallery and pass through a semicircular antechamber into the living room; the library and dining room are to the left and right. To highlight the grandness of these amply proportioned spaces, with their French windows looking south toward Union Square, we opened them up to one another with axial, ten-foot-high doors, producing a glamorous, Gallic enfilade.

Decoratively, each space manifests an individual character. We lined the entry gallery with a rhythmic allée of plaster palms, taken from an eighteenth-century French original, interspersed with vintage mercury-glass mirrors. While the white living room retained its original detailing, the moldings and wall panels received a white gold treatment along their edges, causing them to discreetly shimmer with light. Flanking this space are richly colored chambers with different historical allusions. The dining room was finished in gilded Chinoiserie paneling and featured contemporary allegorical murals in the style of Tiepolo. Conversely, the library is cast as a seventeenth-century Italian studiolo complete with faux decorative marquetry and a frieze with an inscription in Latin.

While the design was conceived in America, both the client and the design team sensed that the finished product required a European touch. Thus, the paneling in the dining room and library and the columns and domed ceiling mural in the master suite were imported from Paris—as were the plasterers, installers, and faux painters and muralists who executed the work.

PREVIOUS PAGES: *The dining room of this San Francisco apartment features gilded Chinoiserie paneling and murals in the style of Tiepolo.*
OPPOSITE: *An allée of plaster palms lines the entry gallery.*

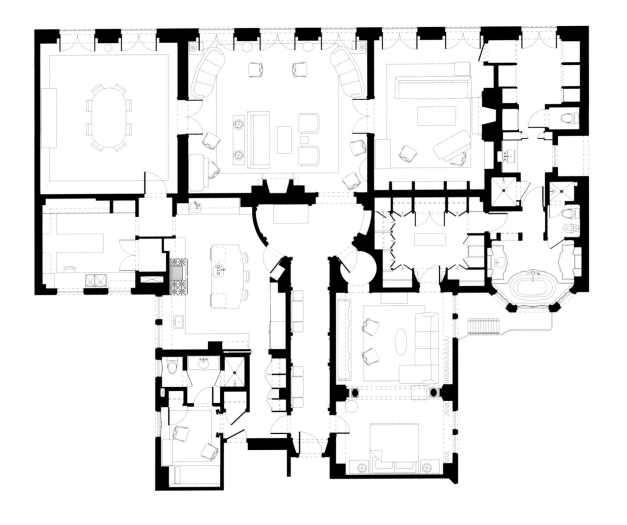

0   5   10   20 ft

PREVIOUS PAGE: *Ten-foot-high axial doors unite the library, living room, and dining room.* ABOVE AND OPPOSITE: *The clients' collection of eighteenth- and nineteenth-century French and Italian furniture adorns the living room, which looks southward toward Union Square.*

LEFT: *A small sitting room off the apartment's powder room is enlivened by Chinese lacquered screens.*

JOHN IKE
Principal

John Ike (center) was raised in Cincinnati, Ohio. He received his bachelor of arts from Colorado College and his master of architecture from the Graduate School of Architecture, Planning and Preservation, Columbia University. With Thomas Kligerman, Ike founded Ike & Kligerman Architects, now Ike Kligerman Barkley Architects. He has a particular interest in interior design and established an interiors department that has become Ike Kligerman Barkley Interiors. Ike travels widely and his design is especially influenced by Italian and Scandinavian precedents. In 2009, he designed a room for the Kips Bay Decorator Show House.

THOMAS A. KLIGERMAN
Principal

Thomas Kligerman (left) was raised in Connecticut and New Mexico. Student years in France and England sparked his interest in the rich history of domestic architecture, gardens, and landscapes. He received his bachelor of arts from Columbia University and his master of architecture from the Yale School of Architecture. Before he and John Ike founded Ike & Kligerman Architects, now Ike Kligerman Barkley Architects, he worked for Robert A. M. Stern Architects. Kligerman is affiliated with a range of professional and architectural organizations and serves on the boards of various charitable and educational institutions, including the Sir John Soane's Museum Foundation.

JOEL BARKLEY
Principal

An architect as well as a watercolorist, Joel Barkley (right) brings a painterly approach to the composition of houses and gardens. He is a native of Chattanooga, Tennessee, and received his bachelor of science from the Georgia Institute of Technology and his master of architecture from Princeton University, where he was awarded the Thesis Prize. He also attended the Ecoles d'Art Américaines de Fontainebleau. Before joining John Ike and Thomas Kligerman to form Ike Kligerman Barkley Architects, he worked for Skidmore, Owings & Merrill; Robert A. M. Stern Architects; and Diller + Scofidio.

JOHN JAMES TOYA
Partner

John Toya developed his love of architecture in his native Chicago and his passion for furniture design at the architecture firm Hancock + Hancock. He received his bachelor of architecture from Iowa State University. In 1996, he joined Ike Kligerman Barkley Architects, and in 2007, he was named a partner. He opened the firm's office in San Francisco in 2008. He is on the board of the Northern California branch of the Institute for Classical Architecture & Classical America.

Monique Agnew
Anna Agoston
Daisy Agustin
Benjamin Alberg
James Angoff
Margaret Arbanas
Stanley Ariza
Eden Baird
Arturo Barcenas
Eric Beaton
Michelle Biancardo
Joshua Bissinger
Lauren Blair
Nancy Boszhardt
Amy Bramwell
Christina Bricker
William Bryant
Audrey Buckley
Maya Caballero
Melissa Campbell
Patricia Cassidy
Ricardo Ceralde
Marcial C. Chao
Ysadora Clarin
Thomas Collins
Andrew Davis
Molly Denver
Joost DeQuack
David Dunn
John Edwards
Alexander Eng★
Amy Epstein
Andrea Federman
Jan Fischer
Amy Flom
Nancy Frank

Reid Freeman
Christina Friedrich
Jeremy Fruchter
Thomas Gay
Lise Gervais
Beth Joy Goldstein
Julia Gorden
Jonathan Graves
Jeremy Greene
Alison Guneyik
Sallie Hambright
Russell Hamilton
Julie Hanselmann
Tracy Harrison
Ann Hawker
Andrew Hayes
Christopher Haynes
Alena Herkiotz
Hans Curtis Herrmann
Francine Hsu-Davis
Lilianna Husseini
Jamill Isaac
Elizabeth Jacks
Carrie Johnson
Victor Jones
Narcissa Jose
Mia Jung
Maki Kawasaki
Elizabeth Kelly
Peter Kilgour
Michael King
Roxana
Klein-Rosenkranz
Kristin Kligerman
Ken Koomalsingh
Louse Krieg

Michael Kudler
Mona LaPorte
Brendan Lee
Pierre LeFlem
Joshua Liu
Gabriel Lloyd
John Lodge
Christopher Lucas
Leslie Mason
David Mathewson
Kenneth McIntyre-Horito
Stephanie Metz
Piotr Milc
Matthew Miles
Mara Miller
Namita Modi
Jennifer Nadler
Dana Napurano
Brian Nee
Thai Minh Nguyen
Tim Nissen
Carol O'Brien
Rachel O'Reilly
Jennifer Overton
Lawrence Owen
Sabrina Pagani
George Perkins
Milan Petkovic
Jeremiah Reilly
Daniel Relyea
Theresa Ricci-Armatowski
Britton Rogers
Nathaniel Rogers
Courtney Rombough
Martin Russocki

Anthony Saccento
Allison Santarossa
Fatima Saqib
Nancy Sato
Ershade Schahangi
Jonathan Schecter
Leo Schneidewind
Wesley Schwartz
Monique Singletary
Scott Skipworth
Christian Standke
Sarah Stehli-Howell
Sopheline Suparman
Susan Tang
Lisa Tasso
Marybeth Tormey
Edna Tricarico
Anna Voeller
Susan Vreeland
Andrea Wang
Kevin Wegner
Carrie Weinstein
Charles Wermers
Stanley Wong
Scott Wood
Quinn Yang
Chongkul Yi
Khadem Zaved

Senior Associate★
Associate

PROJECT CREDITS

ARTS AND CRAFTS COTTAGE
Michigan, 2003

GENERAL CONTRACTOR:
Thomas Sebold & Associates, Inc.

LANDSCAPE ARCHITECT:
Morgan Wheelock Inc.

INTERIOR DESIGNER:
Peter Kilgour Design

PHOTOGRAPHER:
Peter Aaron/ESTO

SHINGLISH COUNTRY HOUSE
New Jersey, 1993

GENERAL CONTRACTOR:
William Cook Custom Homes

LANDSCAPE ARCHITECT:
Steven R. Krog Landscape Architect, P.C.

PHOTOGRAPHER:
Peter Aaron/ESTO

LOOKOUT HOUSE
Fairfield County, Connecticut, 2004

GENERAL CONTRACTOR:
Cornerstone Contracting Corp.

LANDSCAPE ARCHITECT:
Steven R. Krog Landscape Architect, P.C.

PHOTOGRAPHER:
Peter Aaron/ESTO

WOODLAND RAMBLE
Redding, Connecticut, 1998

GENERAL CONTRACTOR:
Frank Talcott, Inc.

INTERIOR DESIGNER:
Renee O'Leary Interiors

PHOTOGRAPHER:
Peter Aaron/ESTO

GREEN SPRINGS FARM
Louisa, Virginia, 2004

GENERAL CONTRACTOR:
Gibson/Magerfield Corp.

INTERIOR DESIGNER:
Renee O'Leary Interiors

PHOTOGRAPHER:
Durston Saylor Photography

CLASSICAL HOUSE
New Jersey, 1999

GENERAL CONTRACTOR:
Frank Valente & Son Custom Builders, Inc.

LANDSCAPE ARCHITECT:
Steven R. Krog Landscape Architect, P.C.

PHOTOGRAPHER:
Peter Aaron/ESTO

ROCKY MOUNTAIN RETREAT
Continental Divide, 2005

Photographer:
Peter Aaron/ESTO

MODERNIST CASINO
New Jersey, 1996

PHOTOGRAPHER:
Peter Aaron/ESTO

CLIFFTOP VILLA
New Jersey, 1999

GENERAL CONTRACTOR:
Carpenter Construction

PHOTOGRAPHER:
Peter Aaron/ESTO

HAWAIIAN LONGHOUSE
Maui, Hawaii, 2004

GENERAL CONTRACTOR:
Trend Builders, LLC

LANDSCAPE ARCHITECT:
Parker Gardens, Ltd.

PHOTOGRAPHER:
Peter Aaron/ESTO

TROPICAL SPLIT-LEVEL
Kaanapali, Hawaii, 2006

GENERAL CONTRACTOR:
Dixon Homes, Inc.

LANDSCAPE ARCHITECT:
Chris Hart & Partners, Inc.

INTERIOR DESIGNER:
Ron Wilson Designer

PHOTOGRAPHER:
Peter Aaron/ESTO

SHINGLE STYLE BEACH HOUSE
Eastern Long Island, 2000

GENERAL CONTRACTOR:
John C. Meyer & Sons, Inc.

LANDSCAPE ARCHITECT:
Steven R. Krog Landscape Architect, P.C.

PHOTOGRAPHER:
Peter Aaron/ESTO

BEACH RETREAT
Cabo San Lucas, Mexico, 2009

GENERAL CONTRACTOR:
Constructora Malver

LANDSCAPE ARCHITECT:
E Group, Inc.

PHOTOGRAPHER:
Peter Aaron/ESTO

NORMAN HOUSE ON THE SOUND
Greenwich, Connecticut, 2004

GENERAL CONTRACTOR:
Hobbs, Inc.

LANDSCAPE ARCHITECT:
Steven R. Krog Landscape Architect, P.C.

INTERIOR DESIGNER:
Michael LaRocca

PHOTOGRAPHER:
Durston Saylor Photography

COMPOUND IN THE DUNES
New England, 2008

PHOTOGRAPHER:
Peter Aaron/ESTO

VILLA ON THE ATLANTIC
New Jersey, 2004

GENERAL CONTRACTOR:
Kay Jay Homes, Ltd.

PHOTOGRAPHER:
Peter Aaron/ESTO

MODERN DUPLEX
New York, New York, 2006

GENERAL CONTRACTOR:
Frank M. DeBono Construction Corp.

PHOTOGRAPHER:
Durston Saylor Photography

RIVER OAKS TOWNHOUSE
Houston, Texas, 2005

GENERAL CONTRACTOR:
Tynes Sparks Building Corp.

LANDSCAPE ARCHITECT:
Ruckel/Dillon/Wright, Inc.

INTERIOR DESIGNER:
Michael J. Siller Interiors

PHOTOGRAPHER:
Durston Saylor Photography

LOFT IN TRIBECA
New York, New York, 2000

GENERAL CONTRACTOR:
Pattern Millwork, Inc.

PHOTOGRAPHER:
Durston Saylor Photography

WEDGE LOFT
New York, New York, 2000

GENERAL CONTRACTOR:
Frank M. DeBono Construction Corp.

PHOTOGRAPHER:
Durston Saylor Photography

ANTIQUARIAN'S APARTMENT
San Francisco, California, 2008

GENERAL CONTRACTOR:
Scott & Warner Builders, Inc.

INTERIOR CONSULTANT:
Ann Getty & Associates

PHOTOGRAPHER:
Steven Brooke Studios, Inc.

ACKNOWLEDGMENTS

In our architecture practice, we have years of experience in design and construction. But when it came to producing a book, we were novices. We are grateful for the efforts of the many people, some directly involved, others more remote, who helped bring this project to fruition.

Our highest thanks go to Paige Rense, who brought many of these projects to the pages of *Architectural Digest*. For bringing our firm before a large and important audience, we are forever grateful. We also thank other members of the *AD* staff: Margaret Dunne, James Huntington, Therese Bissell, Wendy Moonan, and Jeffrey Simpson.

At The Monacelli Press, we are grateful to Gianfranco Monacelli for his support and encouragement. Additionally we thank Elizabeth White for overseeing the fine production and Nicolas Rojas for his help in publicity, the lifeline for any book. We are most deeply indebted to our editor, Andrea Monfried. Andrea's belief in this monograph, keen ideas, and clear vision were the cornerstones of this effort.

We offer appreciation to writer Marc Kristal, who was able to decipher our tangled thoughts and turn them into clear prose. His interviews and patient rewrites as our ideas evolved shaped the text in this book. Designer Doug Turshen created a crisp, clean, and bold design; Doug and his associate, David Huang, brought our projects alive. To our ace photographers Peter Aaron, Durston Saylor, and Steven Brooke, thank you. The brilliant images in this book are the windows through which our work is seen.

We thank Robert A. M. Stern, whose lessons in the design studio, mentorship in the office, professional example, and friendship guide many aspects of our world view and practice. Jill Cohen is the ideal agent—she promoted and organized us, taught us about the business side of books, and patiently shepherded us through the world of publishing. We thank our longtime friend and book savant Cynthia Conigliaro of Archivia Books. Likewise, we acknowledge Keith Granet for his insight on constantly improving our firm.

We are grateful to the talented and dedicated employees who have worked in our office during our first twenty years. Their work has made possible the houses displayed on these pages. In particular, the following people contributed to this book: Arturo Barcenas, Jamill Isaac, Gabriel Lloyd, Christopher Lucas, Nathaniel Rogers, Courtney Rombough, and Scott Skipworth. We could not have produced this book without the dedication and enthusiasm of Ysadora Clarin, who tracked the myriad photographs, text drafts, and details with grace and good humor. Our senior associate, Alexander Eng, deserves our deepest appreciation for his extraordinary talent, drawing ability, insight, and spot-on intuition.

We thank our clients. Without them, we would be daydreaming about the history of the built world and gazing at books on other architects. We are truly grateful.

Finally, Thomas Kligerman thanks Kristin, Rebecca, Katherine, and Magdalen, who make all possible and worthwhile. Joel Barkley thanks Ann McKenzie Aiken, who allowed him to pry his way into the world of architecture. John Ike thanks Kathy, Andy, Emily, and Sally, who are his greatest treasures.